An important book in a very
clumsy, incompetent translation.

Unity of the Churches

Unity of the Churches

AN ACTUAL POSSIBILITY

HEINRICH FRIES
and
KARL RAHNER

Translated by
Ruth C. L. Gritsch and Eric W. Gritsch

FORTRESS PRESS
Philadelphia

PAULIST PRESS
New York/Ramsey

Library of Congress Cataloging in Publication Data

Fries, Heinrich.
Unity of the churches—an actual possibility.

Bibliography: p.
1. Christian union. I. Rahner, Karl, 1904–
II. Title.
BX8.2.F6813 1985   262'.0011   84–48481
ISBN 0–8006–1820–3 (Fortress)
ISBN 0–8091–2671–0 (Paulist)

K905G84   Printed in the United States of America   1–1820

Contents

Introduction to the English Edition

The story of the church in the twentieth century may well be told in the future in terms of the ecumenical movement. Since the early years of this century, this movement, believed by many to be a gift of the Spirit, has with ever-increasing force urged the churches to put aside their polemics of the past, to rediscover and express visibly the unity they share, and to affirm those diversities that enrich the entire Christian tradition.

The aspirations of the ecumenical movement have resulted in some notable achievements dating from the Edinburgh Missionary Conference of 1910 to the conferences of "Life and Work" and "Faith and Order," and on to the formation of the World Council of Churches in 1948 and to the Second Vatican Council of 1963–65 with its "Decree on Ecumenism." The decades of the 1960s and 1970s saw the emergence of theological dialogue as a useful ecumenical tool to resolve with integrity age-old differences. Many impressive agreements were reached between divided churches which, if accepted by the churches and put into practice, would have brought the churches closer together. The period between 1965 and 1975 was for many individuals an intoxicating moment of ecumenical excitement. The churches seemed to be on the threshold of a new chapter of history when they would realize their oneness, although it was not clear exactly what this would mean. Then after 1975 something happened to the euphoria. New problems arose and difficulties were not all that quickly resolved. It became evident that the road to unity was not going to be as short or smooth as had been envisaged. Some wondered whether the ecumenical movement was in the doldrums. Others feared that it had failed to live up to its promise. For all the meetings, all the papers, and all the words, in practice little seemed to have changed. Although there were increased feelings of good will, and some caricatures had been eliminated, the churches still seemed to be hopelessly divided. They did not exhibit their oneness, and Christian women and men with different denominational labels were unable officially to come together at their Lord's table. The earlier ecumenical euphoria was replaced in many circles by cynicism.

It was this ecumenical situation compounded by a mood of skepticism and atheism in the world that in 1983 prompted Heinrich Fries and Karl Rahner, S.J., two veteran Roman Catholic theologians and ecumenists, to publish *Einigung der Kirchen—reale Möglichkeit* (*Unity of the Churches—An Actual Possibility*) as Volume 100 of the prestigious series *Quaestiones Disputatae*. Heinrich Fries is Professor Emeritus of Fundamental and Ecumenical Theology on the Catholic Theological Faculty of Münich. Karl Rahner, S.J., regarded as one of the leading theologians of this century, was Professor Emeritus of Dogmatics and the History of Doctrine at universities in Austria and West Germany until his death in 1984. They have produced a book of special ecumenical importance. After a careful examination of ecumenical progress, both authors concluded that extensive consensus on the decisive questions of faith could be identified that should allow the mainstream churches to move toward realization of their unity. In an urgent way the book puts the question of unity before the churches and offers concrete steps for accomplishing this unity. It is a product of seasoned scholars, building on the earlier work of the Second Vatican Council, the Faith and Order Commission of the World Council of Churches, dialogues and theological reflection in world confessional families, like the Lutheran World Federation.

Perhaps because the book spoke so directly to the desire of so many Christians, it aroused great interest in Europe. The first printing was quickly sold out and several more printings followed. Considerable attention was given to the book by leading Protestant and Roman Catholic theologians. Its main ideas were examined, discussed, and critiqued, on some occasions with serious debate and disagreement. Leading European ecumenists—among them, Harding Meyer of the Institute for Ecumenical Research in Strasbourg,

Eberhard Jüngel of the University of Tübingen, and Cardinal Joseph Ratzinger, Prefect of the Congregation of the Faith, who is quoted in the volume—have reviewed or commented on the book. Fathers Fries and Rahner did much in Europe to bring the ecumenical discussion out of the abstract and to raise questions of immediate relevance for the churches—questions needing to be addressed by parish priests and ministers, church leaders and theologians.

The authors believe that what is necessary for the unity of the churches is actually possible today. In their opinion, the conditions and presuppositions for accomplishing this unity exist in the churches themselves, but must be seen and expressed. Thus, Fries and Rahner have set forth eight theses which clearly formulate these conditions and presuppositions (see pp. 7–10).

The book includes commentaries explaining the rationale of each of the eight theses along with suggestions for their implementation. The commentaries, which reflect developments within Roman Catholic thought and in the ecumenical scene, especially the dialogues on the Lord's Supper, the ministerial office, the episcopacy, and the papal primacy, are divided between the two authors. Heinrich Fries composed commentaries to theses, I, IVa, V, VI, and VIII; Karl Rahner commented on II, III, IVb, and VII. Both authors assumed responsibility for all eight commentaries.

A critical aspect of the argumentation of the book centers in theses II and IV (see pp. 7 and 8). Together these theses allow for an extensive theological diversity held together by the service of unity, described as the task of the Petrine Office. The present intellectual and political situation is the point of departure for the argument. In the situation of contemporary uncertainty, theology does not speak with the degree of assuredness that it once did. Rahner declares, "If a person withholds an affirmative verdict regarding a true (certainly a possible) proposition, he does not err." (See Commentary on Thesis II, esp. II and III.) Rahner speaks of a "withholding of judgment," "eine Enthaltung eines Urteils" on such propositions and believes that from the point of view of dogma, a unity of the churches is already possible with this kind of epistomological tolerance, "erkenntnistheoretischen Toleranz." (See Commentary on Thesis II, IV.) He states that this condition of epistomological tolerance presently exists within the Roman Catholic Church. When the central ecumenical intent is not grasped, such explanations are easily open to misunderstanding and opposition. They can be interpreted to mean that there can be differences between churches, even involving misunderstanding of the faith, which do not raise questions about unity or agreement in faith. Probably part of the difficulty is the term "withholding of judgment." It suggests a skepticism that is false to Rahner's intent, for in the final analysis he and his co-author do wish a judgment. "What is required is that the confessional specificity in the practice of one confession is not contrary to the Gospel and that therefore it must not be condemned or rejected." (See Commentary on Thesis VI, II.) Debate will probably continue about the usefulness of Thesis II and its commentary and this will affect the estimate of the worth of the entire volume, but a final judgment of this thesis should be made in the context of all eight theses.

Notwithstanding specific points that could be assisted by further clarification or reformulation, this volume by Heinrich Fries and Karl Rahner merits serious attention by all concerned with, or involved in, the present ecumenical movement. It places sharp and direct questions to us all. The European reception and debate of this work substantiate this contention. Fortress Press deserves our gratitude for making this significant publication available to English-speaking readers in the excellent translation of Ruth and Eric Gritsch.

WILLIAM G. RUSCH

Translators' Preface

We have tried to preserve the linguistic virtuosity of the authors in our translation. Our decision to be as literal as possible was inevitable, since this book is a very carefully nuanced argument for Christian unity, and therefore every word counts.

A few words required particular attention because of the context of the authors' argumentation, as well as their significance. Therefore *real* was translated as "actual" rather than "real" or "realistic"; *Teilkirche* was rendered as "partner church," even though Vatican II documents refer to "particular churches." Some terms appeared with variations in the original, which we attempted to follow: *Amt* as "ministerial office," but *kirchliches Amt* as "ecclesiastical office," and *Ämter* as "offices"; *Grosskirche* as "mainline church," but *Grosse Kirche* as "large church."

We used official translations of the ecumenical documents quoted by the authors. In cases of variations between our text and the documents quoted, however, we opted for the authors' rendition. English titles are cited in the notes in addition to the sources listed by the authors. Biblical quotations are taken from the Revised Standard Version.

Ruth C. L. Gritsch and Eric W. Gritsch

June 1984

Introduction

The unity of the Church is the commandment of the Lord of the Church, who will demand from the leaders of the churches an accounting as to whether or not they have really done everything possible in this matter. This unity is a matter of life or death for Christendom at a time when faith in God and His Christ are most seriously threatened by a worldwide militant atheism, and by a relativistic skepticism even in those countries where atheism is not yet a state religion. Today, where it is no longer supported by European colonialism, Christianity can no longer afford to encounter peoples and cultures to whom it still wishes to convey its message—so far almost in vain—in its splintered and ruptured state.

The lack of the great unity of the churches also signifies, among Christians themselves, a constant weakening of their courage of faith and of their confidence, particularly since there are no longer any countries and regions where what is Christian could be socially and culturally obvious to the general public and thus support and facilitate the Christian faith. There may still be some enclaves where what is Christian has preserved its old plausibility from the outside. It is also conceivable that many church leaders in all communions (most of them stemming from these enclaves) do not yet have any spontaneous and radical perception of the urgency of the ecumenical task, even if they are of good will and theoretically acknowledge this task. But, on the whole, all churches and Christian communities today exist in a situation in which the ecumenical task has become an urgent matter of survival for Christianity and the churches, the high priority of which can be seen ever more clearly.

But if one must define the actual ecumenical situation today, one can well say the following: We have an ecumenism of adjuring words which can hardly be surpassed in intensity. During his visit to Ger-

1

many, Pope John Paul II declared, "I mean to serve the cause of unity. I mean to take any road on which, after the experiences of centuries and millennia, Christ is guiding us to the unity of that flock of which He alone is the one and sure good shepherd."

If one compares these words to the reality of practice, especially in the Catholic church, one can state without a doubt that more has happened and more has been achieved ecumenically in the last three decades than in previous centuries—above all, through the impulse of the Second Vatican Council and through the Würzburg Synod in the German Federal Republic. This cannot and need not be described in detail here; it can be assumed. But it should never be forgotten when taking stock. It is cause for joy and gratitude.

On the other hand, there is an increasing tendency not to move outside the framework established at the Second Vatican Council, and especially not to go beyond the limitations it set—particularly concerning the questions of the ministerial office (including the papacy) and of the Eucharist. Every attempt to do so is received with displeasure. There is greater concern to guard the homogeneity of the confessional interior space than to attempt further ecumenical rapprochements. Occasionally one even gets the impression that the bar to ecumenical possibilities keeps being raised to higher levels. At present, one swings back toward the status quo, and comforts oneself with the fact that the relationship between the churches and the confessions has become significantly better and friendlier, better and friendlier than ever before. No one can argue against that; but the question is whether this accomplishes the ecumenical task and discharges the ecumenical responsibility.

Further initiatives are dismissed with the words, "The time is not yet ripe," "We are not ready yet." The "already" and "not yet" are maintained, and this situation is rehearsed. The resulting tension, though painful, is to be endured for the sake of honesty, but also for the sake of not letting the ecumenical commitment abate.

That leaves only the question, who is it, and what is the time which one claims is not yet ripe? Are not we ourselves the time, as Augustine says? And will time not consist of what we make of it and of how we shape it? And how much time will be allowed for the "not yet"? Can we think in terms of centuries, as we did earlier? Does not time then run away? And finally, who determines whether or when time is ripe? Are not the signs of the time a reality that must also be considered theologically?

Given the situation, the following modes of behavior are revealed in practice: individual groups—driven by ecumenical impatience—practice on their own, at their own risk, and on their own responsibility things that are officially and generally considered to be still impossible such as, for example, celebrating open communion. They take eventual conflicts with official church leaders into account, and appeal to an "obedience in advance." They already practice now what everyone desires, what everyone prays for, and what should be a goal for everyone someday. They believe their actions are justified on the basis of long ecumenical experience, like mixed marriages. They define the unrest in the church, which stems from this conduct, as salutary unrest necessary for the sake of life in the Church.

Another reaction appears as ecumenical resignation and enervation. One gives up hope that there will be any change in the status quo, or that any further steps forward will be taken. One ends one's ecumenical commitment—which can lead to sheer passivity, indifference, and lack of interest. Others welcome this development and think that a focus of unrest in the Church has thus been eliminated, and that precisely this serves the peace.

Still others declare that ecumenism has run its course, is passé, and no longer moves anyone, considering the overwhelming, far greater world problems which are expressed in the words "justice," "peace," and "freedom," in the reconciliation of nations—especially of the poor and the rich nations.

One cannot be happy about all of these possible and actual modes of behavior. If ecumenical impatience leads to conflict in the Church, or if it makes itself independent, it cannot be desirable, for the conflict also damages ecumenism. Ecumenism can only attain its goal as a movement of the whole Church. There are certainly a few disagreements, tensions, and differences in ways of thinking involved, but they should be endured as marks of life, and they should be resolved in mutual dialogical endeavor without anxiety. Otherwise, the danger of a third confession cannot be avoided.

Ecumenical resignation is really an internal contradiction. To abandon the goal of ecumenism and to end one's ecumenical commitment is a violation of the mandate and mission of the Church as expressed in the testament of Jesus, "That they may become perfectly one . . . so that the world may know that thou hast sent me" (John 17:23).

To leave ecumenism behind as an outmoded phase in order to solve more important world problems means to abandon possibilities, forces, and impulses that are indispensable to today's world precisely because of the experiences and gifts of the Church.

All this is historical and church-historical background for the "controversial issue" we present here. Our attempt begins with the conviction formulated by the Würzburg Synod:

> The ecumenical task tolerates no postponement. The favorable hour, given by the Lord of all time, must not be neglected. Already there are disquieting signs of enervation of the ecumenical will which found its epoch-making expression at the Second Vatican Council. So much the more are responsible people in parish, diocese, and world Church called to hone their ecumenical consciences. Ecumenical orientation must become the new style of the Church.

In addition, the separation of the churches is a violation of the testament of Jesus Christ and the apostles, and moreover constitutes a continuing scandal which renders the churches themselves—and their message to the world of today—less and less credible. We become guilty all over again if the separation of the churches does not distress us to the greatest extent and does not require an all-out effort of us.

The demand to set priorities for general behavior will always be made in the reality of human existence and thus also of the Church. It does not matter whether, by the very nature of the case, the priority proves to be valid for all time, or whether a choice is required of a human being who must choose but is incapable of wanting everything at once or with equal intensity. Where a certain priority is fixed, it may of course be pursued only with legitimate means— but also with all such means. In fact, one cannot expect, in the reality of human existence, that the legitimacy of the means to be used is absolutely obvious to everyone, or that it is established with metaphysical certainty and clarity. In human existence, it must often

4

suffice to have a reasonable moral certainty regarding the legitimacy of the means to be used—especially when neglecting to strive carries not greater but rather less moral legitimacy.

We hold that the ecumenical task has, and must have, one of the highest priorities for the responsibility and work of the Church. This priority determines the reflections to be presented in this volume. They do not intend to pursue academic ecumenical theology. They are (even when they want to be dispassionate) more a cry of distress from Christians who have the impression that no progress is being made in this matter. They do not emanate from the opinion that the influential church leaders do not have honest intentions or do not sense their responsibilities in this matter. But even very intelligent, quite irreproachable, and very responsible people can underestimate the urgency, and particularly the realizability, of a required task; they can find themselves paralyzed by a seeming impossibility to make real progress in a mandated matter; they can think they have very good reasons to judge other matters to be even more urgent. One example is the efforts to achieve governmental abolition of slavery at the beginning of the nineteenth century. Did not many Christians and important church leaders underestimate the urgency of this human task, and was not Cardinal Charles M. Lavigerie a rare exception at the beginning?[1]

During all great historical transitions from one period to another, convictions must first be created laboriously in the struggle against old plausibilities, and intricate proof must be adduced, in almost endless speeches, for things which afterward appear quite self-evident. How shrewdly, for example, did most Catholic theologians wage their bitter fight for 150 years—until the Second Vatican Council—against the thesis regarding freedom of conscience and against the law which an erring Catholic invokes against the Catholic state religion! When large-scale concrete historical decisions are at stake, a matter is never completely clear *prior* to the decision, nor does it obtain unanimous consensus, and yet actions are taken and decisions are made. Such a decision must be justified by reason and must be appropriate to the matter under discussion before it is made. But a problem can also be tabled due to sheer cautiousness and scruple, qualities cherished by those who are conservatively (not admitted, of course) satisfied with the existing situation, and do not at all want it seriously changed. Thus not-deciding can have worse consequences than deciding wrongly.

But our attempt is also carried by the conviction that what is necessary is today also *actually possible*. The conditions and presuppositions to accomplish it exist in the churches themselves; they must be seen and expressed. They are being presented in theses illustrated with appropriate commentaries.

The commentaries have been divided between the two authors. Although both authors are responsible for all of them, they disclose the individual literary style of each. We do not think this to be a disadvantage. The commentaries to theses I, IVa, V, VI, and VIII were written by Heinrich Fries; theses II, III, IVb, and VII were commented upon by Karl Rahner.

We anticipate the reproach that our proposal for how church unity could be realized in fact merely seeks another form of the World Council of Churches. But we are convinced that such an objection is unjustified, for we clearly demand a unity of the churches in the faith, even though we think of this unity of faith—on the basis of the spiritual situation of today—as more differentiated than had been supposed in earlier ecumenical reflections.

This also means that we do not simply leave the present status quo of the churches unchanged; rather, we speak in favor of their renewal, and we hope for renewal. This signifies a way and a movement. We state conditions for an actual possibility.

Naturally there are many other individual themes needing further reflection in order to solve the ecumenical task, which we do not deal with here. But we think that those questions too can be solved along the same lines we are following here.

The Theses

What short answer can we give when we are asked whether a unity of faith and church could be achieved in the foreseeable future among the large Christian churches? A difficult question, which most Christians probably answer with no. But we say yes, under the following conditions—which seem to us to be realizable in a relatively short time, if one perceives that this unity is such a radical obligation coming from Jesus that one has the courage to postpone a number of rather significant scruples. These, then, are the conditions we mean, although it may be that we have forgotten a few.

I

The fundamental truths of Christianity, as they are expressed in Holy Scripture, in the Apostles' Creed, and in that of Nicaea and Constantinople are binding on all partner churches of the one Church to be.

II

Beyond that, a realistic principle of faith should apply: Nothing may be rejected decisively and confessionally in one partner church which is binding dogma in another partner church. Furthermore, beyond Thesis I no explicit and positive confession in one partner church is imposed as dogma obligatory for another partner church. This is left to a broader consensus in the future. This applies especially to authentic but undefined doctrinal decrees of the Roman church, particularly with regard to ethical questions. According to this principle only that would be done which is already practice in every church today.

III

In this one Church of Jesus Christ, composed of the uniting churches, there are regional partner churches which can, to a large

7

extent, maintain their existing structures. These partner churches can also continue to exist in the same territory, since this is not impossible in the context of Catholic ecclesiology or the practice of the Roman church, as, for example, in Palestine.

IVa

All partner churches acknowledge the meaning and right of the Petrine service of the Roman pope to be the concrete guarantor of the unity of the Church in truth and love.

IVb

The pope, for his part, explicitly commits himself to acknowledge and to respect the thus agreed upon independence of the partner churches. He declares (by human right, *iure humano*) that he will make use of his highest teaching authority (ex cathedra), granted to him in conformity with Catholic principles by the First Vatican Council, only in a manner that conforms juridically or in substance to a general council of the whole Church, just as his previous ex cathedra decisions have been issued in agreement and close contact with the whole Catholic episcopate.

V

All partner churches, in accordance with ancient tradition, have bishops at the head of their larger subdivisions. The election of a bishop in these partner churches need not be done according to the normally valid manner in the Roman Catholic church. (The new Roman *Canon Law* also mentions ways of appointing a bishop other than through the pope's free choice. See can. 377, par. 1.)[2]

VI

The partner churches live in mutual fraternal exchange of all aspects of their life, so that the previous history and experience of the churches separated earlier can become effective in the life of the other partner churches.

VII

Without prejudice to the judgment of another church concerning the theological legitimacy of the existing ministerial office in the separated churches, all partner churches commit themselves henceforth to conduct ordinations with prayer and the laying on of hands, so that acknowledging them will present no difficulty for the Roman Catholic partner church either.

VIII

There is pulpit and altar fellowship between the individual partner churches.

We do not know whether we have forgotten any conditions and presuppositions for a faith and church unity which one side or another might consider irrevocable and equally fundamental. But we do think that the conditions listed can be accepted in principle by all the churches—including the Roman Catholic church—given the state of theology in all the confessions. Of course, the fulfillment of these conditions would still require many reflections and many individual agreements on all sides. But if one wants to transcend the verbal assertions of all the large Christian confessions that, in accordance with Jesus' commandment, demand the unity of the Christian churches, then, in our opinion, one should finally determine more exactly, more concretely, and in joint reflection, those conditions under which each existing church considers a speedy unity possible. When establishing such conditions, each church would have the duty and responsibility—derived from the commandment of Jesus—to expand its own conditions no more than is clearly commanded by its own religious conviction of what is important to salvation. This should be done with real courage, and some perhaps weighty doubts should be left aside.

Each historical tradition and custom contains, besides its good moments, a moment of inertia which prevents a society, and therefore also a church, from moving quickly into the future which God has intended for it and requires of it. We think that all the churches act with too much tactical caution in the quest for actual unity. They do not really come out courageously with declarations as to what the conditions are under which they are really prepared to unite with other churches, even with sacrifice. Each church waits for the other church to take the initiative and to express very clearly what it could truly not relinquish without, in its own religious conscience, incurring guilt before God. Nor do they express what does not belong thereto and can, therefore, be relinquished in order to fulfill Jesus' commandment.

We ourselves are pessimistic with regard to the question of whether the officials of all these churches can bring about unity in the near future, even though we have no right to deny all of them their good intentions. But we are convinced—and to that extent optimistic—that there is an objective possibility today for creating a satisfactory and speedy church unity.

Commentary to the Theses

THESIS I

The fundamental truths of Christianity, as they are expressed in Holy Scripture, in the Apostles' Creed, and in that of Nicaea and Constantinople are binding on all partner churches of the one Church to be.

I

The one Church to be is a possibility only if it is a *community of faith.* "Faith" does not mean just any form of religiosity whatever. Faith is not a religious act of some sort which is neutral toward a possible content; rather, it is a faith having very specific, concretely describable contents to which faith is linked and by which faith finds its bearings.

These contents are antecedent to both the individual believer and the community of faith. Neither an individual nor a community drafted or produced them. Instead, these contents are, for believers, what they have accepted and received, what has been given and said to them, and what to them has become event and actuality in history. For faith, receiving takes primacy over doing. This does not exclude but rather includes the fact that what has been said in faith to the person and what has been received by that person bears an inner relation to the person. This person is disposed to be a believer, also and precisely in the sense of the Christian faith. Nor does it exclude the fact that the actuality of what is believed is being completed in the believers themselves, and that the believer integrates faith within himself as a part of himself. In other words: Christian faith does not mean the alienation but the graciously given fulfillment of human existence.

This basic structure of the Christian faith obviously has something to do with the fact that the individual receives his faith by way of the community of faith and of the believers; and that the individual comes to faith by joining this antecedent community. This is clearly demonstrated in the "dialogue" in the baptismal rite: the question "What do you desire from the Church?" is answered with "Faith." The community therefore assumes primacy over the individual in the realm of Christian faith because the recipient and carrier of the original message was from the very beginning a "people" of believers and not an isolated individual. But again this does not

13

exclude but rather includes the fact that the individual who is sustained by the community also helps to sustain this community with his faith.

Holy Scripture is the record of the Christian faith described here according to its content and accomplishment. It is the varied fallout in written form of the faith of a community which orients itself by Jesus Christ: by His person, by His word, by His work, by what in Him became an event culminating in death and resurrection. The result of this was that the mystery of the person of Jesus Christ was revealed: Jesus is the Christ, He is the Lord, He is the Son of God in a sense reserved entirely to Him, He is the Redeemer and Savior of the world. Thus the result is also a new situation: the proclaiming Jesus becomes the proclaimed Christ; the believing Jesus becomes the believed Christ.

Holy Scripture, above all the New Testament, is the testimony of the first believers, the testimony of the first witnesses—actually of the proclamation and faith of the apostles, the ones called by Jesus, the witnesses to the resurrection of Jesus—and thus it is the testimony of those sent into all the world by Jesus the Christ, of those filled with His Spirit. Holy Scripture is the record of the faith of the Church at its inception. This is not only a chronological but also a normative origin, a standard for all that is to come, yet simultaneously critical of the tradition. "The river does not rise above its source" (John H. Newman) applies to this origin.

Thus what is to come is understood as the history of the effect and interpretation of this origin. But this also means that the effect and interpretation of the origin cannot be merely a mechanical repetition of it; rather, it means an ever-deeper initiation into the origin by way of lively intercourse with it.

Since, in the testimony of Holy Scripture, the message of Jesus the Christ, of the Lord and Savior, is proclaimed as a message to all of humanity, to both Jews and Gentiles, the word of Holy Scripture must always be transmitted anew and translated anew—in a fashion faithful to its origin and appropriate to the situation—for people of different times, cultures, languages, and points of view. And it must always be transmitted and translated anew in the context and according to the formulation of questions of a given historical period. Only in this way can the message of the gospel become and remain the normative and liberating word for humanity. The content of the message expressed in Holy Scripture is not changed, but it takes on new perspectives. For its own sake, it can assume a new language mode and yet remain precisely itself. To be sure, the river does not rise above its source, but in the river can be discerned the abundance which is connected with the source and origin. This is the reason for a history of faith.

But the result of what has been said is also: everything that is to come must be responsible to the origin and must, as it were, be capable of reflecting it.

This normative origin testified to in Holy Scriptures is antecedent to the community of faith, the Church, throughout its two-thousand-year history up to the present time, and is at the same time the enduring basis of its life. Without this basis, the Church would lose its foundation and the particularity of its determination and mission. Thus the question will always be whether and how this origin has been preserved and kept alive in the course of history and through history, and whether the claim of every Christian church to have remained true to the origin has been fulfilled.

II

But why are the fundamental truths of Christianity—as they are also proclaimed in the Apostles' Creed and in that of Nicaea and Constantinople—now binding on all partner churches of the one Church?

We have said that the normative origin of Christian faith given in Holy Scripture contains a history of its effects and brings it forth. The so-called Creeds, the basic form of which can be found again in the New Testament (Rom. 10:9; 1 Cor. 12:3; 15:2-5; 1 Tim. 2:5; 3:16), are among these historical effects; and the Old Testament already contains models of them (Deut. 6:20-25; 26:4-9). The Creed is faith's response; it is possible where faith as response exists.

The Creed is response to response. It is the voicing, the promulgation of response. The Creed is linked to the content of faith, but does not articulate all its details; rather, it articulates the contents in their concentrated center, and therefore expresses the fundamental truths of Christian faith. The primary place of the Creed is in baptism as sacrament of faith and in worship service—more accurately, in the congregation's response to the proclaimed and received gospel. In this form, the Creed is not only an expression of commitment but also an act of honor, of praise, and of glorification.

The Creed permits the possibility of rendering account for the living hope within every Christian (1 Peter 3:15). It is at the same time the way in which the Christian faith delimits itself in face of what it itself is not, and in face of the possible distortions it may encounter. Thus the Creed, linked to the center of faith, expresses "the distinction of what is Christian." Furthermore, the Creed draws attention to the fact that faith is not a private matter; rather, it turns toward the public, toward the public community of faith itself, which has its support and basis of existence in the Creed. But it also turns toward the public world, which can view Christian faith with neutrality, but which can also be hostile to it. Thus it can happen that he who confesses his faith is brought to trial, that he must there acknowledge his confession, that he must be ready to suffer repulsion, persecution, and even death for the sake of this confession. The confessor thus stands in succession to him about whom 1 Timothy said that Jesus Christ gave testimony before Pontius Pilate "in the good confession" (1 Tim. 6:13).

The *Apostolicum* (Apostles' Creed) stems from Rome; it was formulated during the second and third centuries in connection with the act of baptism. Its older form was a dialogue of question and answer annexed to Matt. 28:19 about faith in God the Father, in Jesus Christ the Son of God, and in the Holy Spirit. In the course of time, amplifications of the basic Trinitarian arrangement were added to it, and the question-and-answer scheme was replaced by a continuous text. Due to the particular position occupied by the church of Rome with regard to the whole Christian West, the baptismal confession (the Apostles' Creed) of the city of Rome was able to attain general acceptance in the whole Latin-speaking region. The final form of the text was set by Charlemagne, who endorsed its acceptance in his empire. The name *Apostolicum* is derived from the legend that each of the twelve articles into which this creed was divided was written by one of the twelve apostles.[3]

This creed of the city of Rome remained unknown in the East. It was not prayed there, which demonstrates the limitation of the *Apostolicum.* Nevertheless, the *Apostolicum* and its content is part of the foundation of the Christian churches in the West; it has become an essential element of the Reformation Confessional writings.

The Confession of Nicaea (325) and Constantinople (381) achieves greater significance because of the limitation of the *Apostolicum,* for it is the confession of the unseparated churches in both the East and the West. Whether this confession was adopted in its fixed formulation, or whether the church council in Constantinople wrote it, is of secondary importance. Even though both confessions stem from the Eastern church (not a single Western bishop was represented at the Council of Constantinople) the Constantinople confession, which is based on the Nicaean confession and elaborates on it, was received by the whole Church—not because of its juridical formulation, but because of the quality of its content and its conformity to Scripture, above all because of the fundamental truths of the Christian faith expressed in it.

The Confession of Nicaea and Constantinople is therefore a clamp which still holds the meanwhile-separated churches together. At the same time, it exhorts to ecclesiological communion, for which it is the historically established presupposition and condition.

The confessions of Nicaea (325) and Constantinople (381) belong together; indeed, they are as one. Constantinople used Nicaea as basis and considered itself a supplement rather than a substitute of Nicaea. The Church's faith in Jesus Christ found its authoritative formulation in Nicaea through its expression of the Son's equal substance with the Father. The Creed of Constantinople supplemented the christological assertions with affirmations regarding the divinity of the Holy Spirit. The Confession of Nicaea and Constantinople received by the churches is thus the authentic presentation of the Church's faith in the Trinitarian God who is not a substitute for monotheism but is instead its Christian form.

These two confessions present the totality of the fundamental truths of the Christian faith. And if one considers the concrete affirmations and descriptions which are related to faith in God the Father, Son, and Spirit, then one can say that both confessions—

which are as one—are not only the conclusion of a turbulent history of the faith, but also contain a whole theology in shorthand: doctrine of God, Christology, pneumatology, soteriology, and ecclesiology.[4] The Council of Chalcedon did not present a creed of its own. It "once again received the faith of the 150 fathers in Constantinople who confirmed and elucidated the faith of the 318 fathers of Nicaea." Thus the confession of Nicaea and Constantinople attained the highest and most binding rank, that is "this one, authoritative, central creed, bearing all others, is accepted as a two-in-one; moreover, it is accepted without criticism and without contradiction."[5]

The Eastern church considers the Creed of Nicaea and Constantinople to be the sign of communion in true faith up to the present day; indeed, it makes the Creed the object of religious veneration and liturgical act of faith, "cultic monument of the Triune God on earth." The same Creed was valued no less highly in the church of the West, even with regard to its position in the liturgy.

The assertion regarding the Holy Spirit proceeding from the Father and the Son (*Filioque*) which was later added in the Western church by the provincial Synod of Braga (675) was the subject of fierce theological controversies. These controversies have not yet been fully resolved, even though solutions, in the ecumenical sense, are being sought at present. However, this episode does not detract from the binding significance to the whole Church of the Creed of Nicaea and Constantinople. It contains irrevocable, irreversible truth in a language conditioned by time; it represents a consensus of the Church which has been maintained throughout history.

This creed was accepted into the confessional writings of the Reformation churches, which claimed to be the exposition of the ancient church faith. This confession also has its place in the worship service of the churches of the Reformation. To "hold on to" the *Credo* of 381 "belongs to the catholicity of the Evangelical church. It would lose its being as Church of Jesus Christ if it no longer accepted or presented the matter formulated in this dogma."[6]

The Confession of Nicaea and Constantinople is the foundation for the basic formula of the World Council of Churches: "The World Council of Churches is a communion of churches which confess the Lord Jesus Christ as God and Savior in accordance with Holy Scripture and therefore strive together to fulfill what they together have been called to do, to the honor of God the Father, Son, and Holy Spirit."

The Declaration devoted to this subject by the General Synod of Bishops in the Federal Republic of Germany sounds similar: "Where churches and ecclesiastical communities confess, in accordance with Scripture, Jesus Christ true God and true human being as sole Mediator of salvation, to the honor of God the Father, Son, and Holy Spirit, a fundamental unity of faith has been given."[7]

The Consultations of the Commission for Faith and Order of the World Council of Churches more and more often and more and more clearly make the Creed of Nicaea and Constantinople the foundation and guide for their ecumenical endeavors. Wolfhart Pannenberg explicitly states that no later confession has superseded the representative force of this confession as obligatory confession for the whole Church of all time, and that this confession cannot be superseded and is definitive. All succeeding traditions and developments must be tested in the light of this confession and must be subordinated to it.[8]

To say this does not mean that this confession needs only to be repeated word for word. Its place in the liturgies of all the churches demands the continuous task of interpretation and responsible exposition. However, this task cannot be accomplished by merely seeking to formulate new creeds suited to the spirit of any one time. Instead, the old creed must be communicated in a manner which remains faithful to its origin and yet is appropriate to the situation. The enduring validity of the Creed of Nicaea and Constantinople is the guarantor of the continuity and identity of the churches throughout time.

The problem of the *Filioque* ("also from the Son") has been taken up again in present ecumenical discussions. Several mediating solutions have been offered. Yves Congar suggests that the teaching office withdraw the *Filioque* under the condition that the Eastern churches concede the nonheretical character of the *Filioque* which can be substantiated on the basis of the New Testament. He added that believers in both churches should be prepared for such a change so that they would be able to accept it.[9] The kind of unity in freedom can be applied to the *Filioque* which we deal with in Thesis II. If the Latin *Filioque* is not rejected by the Eastern churches as heretical (and is understood by them to be interpreted in conformity to their own ancient formulas) then the Latin churches need not conversely demand from the Eastern churches an explicitly formulated confession of the *Filioque* in their confessional writings and in their creeds in the liturgy.

III

One other ecumenical consequence follows from what has been said. Although the fundamental truths of Christian faith have been formulated in the Confession of Nicaea and Constantinople, this does not exclude but instead includes their further interpretation and development, through all those motivations and challenges that determine the history of faith and of theology, and also of dogmas. These developments have justification and legitimation if they can be made to reflect the fundamental truths of the Christian faith and at the same time make clear that they are basically a faithful exposition of them. The principle of "the hierarchy of truths" affirmed in Vatican II—a principle not of selection but of correct interpretation—is important to ecumenical dialogue and can be of decisive help and guidance to it. The hierarchy, the classification of truth, conforms "to the varied manner of its connection to the foundation of the Christian faith."[10]

Beyond this, if it seems conceivable that the "separated churches of Christianity understand their various, and in some cases contradictory, teaching traditions in a new way, as various interpretations of the one faith of the Church, given in the Confession of Nicaea and Constantinople,"[11] then a great ecumenical opportunity has been opened up. Then it would also be possible to test, to explain, and to interpret this variety in light of this common foundation. This should result in a mutual convergence and understanding—as well as mutual correction and assistance—which is guided by that foundation. Indeed, it would surpass by far what is demanded in Thesis II as a presupposition for the unity of faith.

On this basis, and in accordance to this orientation, it should be possible—by ever deeper and more penetrating efforts—to succeed in making a reconciled variety out of the diversities that still seem to have the character of opposition in the church-dividing sense. This brings into view the particular image of the unity of the churches which is not only being discussed in a lively manner all over the world, but which also possesses the promise of real, honest, and nonbetraying realization: the image of a reconciled diversity which simultaneously opposes every kind of monolithic uniformity. At the same time, it signifies the gaining of the Spirit-given gifts and charisms of the churches. This does not, however, exclude other formulations of unity, such as, for example, that of conciliar communion, of unity in diversity.

IV

One final thing should be said: the Creed of Constantinople is in a special fashion the confession to the Holy Spirit, the Lord and Giver of Life. This is also and especially significant for the ecumenical issue. In connection with faith in the Holy Spirit, the *Church becomes the object of faith as ecclesia una, sancta, catholica, et apostolica (the one, holy, catholic, and apostlic Church)*. The "I believe in the Church (*credo ecclesiam*)" corresponds to the "I believe in the Holy Spirit (*credo in Spiritum Sanctum*)." Its meaning for the Church is that it understands itself to be the creature and work of the Spirit who effects the representation of Jesus Christ. The Spirit, in the plenitude of its gifts and charisms, must be the life-giving principle of the Church. The Church must prove itself to be the place of the Spirit's effectiveness, and make room for the Spirit's rule, which blows where, how, and when it wills, especially in the effectiveness of the prophets and saints.

Vatican II describes the Holy Spirit's effectiveness in the Church in these words: Through the power of the Gospel, the Spirit allows the Church to always rejuvenate herself; it renews her constantly, and leads her to complete unification with her bridegroom. In this way the whole Church appears as a people united by the unity of the Father and the Son and the Holy Spirit (Cyprian, Augustine, John of Damascus).[12]

It is more than coincidence that Vatican II states the first mark of belonging to the communion of the Church to be: those "who possess the Spirit of Christ"[13] will be fully incorporated into the communion of the Church. The ministerial office of the Church also considers itself a charism of the Spirit and thereby resists the danger of being merely institution. But the Spirit is not confined to the ministerial office, channeled in such a way as to make it subordinate to the ministerial office.

The Church as creature and sacrament of the Spirit[14] is preserved by the Spirit from petrifying historically or institutionally, and from succumbing to immobility. The Spirit is the guarantee of constantly new fundamental changes and initiatives in the Church. The Spirit is the guarantor for the fact that the Church not holy is but is also always becoming event.

Looking at the Church from the pneumatological aspect means that the Church as creature and sacrament of the Spirit is a *church always to be reformed (ecclesia semper reformanda),* a church just as capable of renewing itself as it has need to do so. The orientations for this renewal are the decisive origins which, besides Holy Scripture, include the ancient church creeds as well as the orientation toward the pertinent historical moment which, according to the council, is a theological location.[15]

Looking at the Church as creature and sacrament of the Spirit means that because it is only sacrament of the Spirit, the Church looks beyond itself and points beyond itself to the world of people to whom it has been sent, and above all to the religions of the world. And it means that the Church acknowledges the rule and work of the Spirit outside itself: in the other Christian and ecclesiastical communities of which Vatican II—in clear contradistinction to the encyclical *"Mystici Corporis"* 1943—declares that the Spirit of God makes use of them to mediate salvation.[16]

The Church as creature and *sacrament* of the Spirit thereby confesses that its future—and with it the future in which the partner churches together will represent the one Church of Jesus—is not totally predictable, cannot be manipulated, and in no way runs only according to the norms known heretofore. Instead, the future, without detriment to the binding commitments of all Christians and churches, is a matter of the unavailability and freedom of the Spirit of God, who, as Creator Spirit, is also repeatedly capable of new

22

creation. The person of Pope John XXIII, the Second Vatican Council, and a variety of charismatic revivals at the present time refer to the work of this Spirit.

It is to be wished that unity of the churches at it already exists in the Spirit of God, in the Spirit of Jesus Christ, as it portrays and shows itself in the fundamental Confession of Nicaea and Constantinople, would create a greater, a more concrete, and a more credible realization than is the case today.

THESIS II

Beyond that, a realistic principle of faith should apply: Nothing may be rejected decisively and confessionally in one partner church which is binding dogma in another partner church. Furthermore, beyond Thesis I no explicit and positive confession in one partner church is imposed as dogma obligatory for another partner church. This is left to a broader consensus in the future. This applies especially to authentic but undefined doctrinal decrees of the Roman church, particularly with regard to ethical questions. According to this principle only that would be done which is already practice in every church today.

After the first thesis regarding the unity of the future Church in faith, the second thesis also deals with the unity of faith as such. On the one hand, it is clear that the unity of faith cannot simply confine itself to the enduring validity of the Apostles' Creed and the Confession of Nicaea and Constantinople. The history of faith, of dogma, and of theology has progressed for almost fifteen hundred years, and the churches which should unite certainly cannot erase this history.

Moreover, the individual churches have undergone different developments in their faith-awareness, which cannot be simply crossed out either. But on the other hand, if the unity of the churches is not to remain a pure utopian or theoretical postulation, unity in faith must be planned in a way which will make allowances for these differing developments and the concomitant dissimilarity in the timing of the churches to be united. This is the problem dealt with in Thesis II.

Beyond what has just been indicated, this thesis also intends to allow for the circumstance that the intellectual and political present of people today has changed so much, in comparison to earlier times, that the *way* the understanding of faith of the existing churches can and must be brought into the one future Church of faith can deviate very much from the only way one could, until now, conceive of unity of faith in the controversies between the churches and confessions. This does not mean that, because of this circumstance, the actual substance of the Christian faith, and that which the existing churches have counted as a "definitive" part of the substance of their faith, should be changed or relinquished.

I

The basic thesis can be made more comprehensible if one can start further back in order to illustrate the intellectual-political situation in which people, and therefore churches too, live today.

This intellectual-political situation in which a human being can live should be clarified. The differences in these situations at various times during the course of history should be made comprehensible. Our present situation should be distinguished from the one in which all previous controversies about church unity have occurred and which at times naturally penetrates into the present we experience ourselves. But, as a result, it is obvious that the characterizations of these situations must turn out unfailingly primitive in their distinction. Furthermore, differences are more clearly worked out than what is enduring and common to these situations, so that one can very easily raise objections to such a description.

But what is to be presented on this subject is probably correct on the whole; and it is of decisive importance to the question of how a unity of faith can even be thought of, let alone demanded.

What does our intellectual-political situation, in which the Christian faith must be affirmed, look like today? How does it compare with the West's intellectual-political situation at the time churches were separating and staying separated?

This difference should be expressed simply and elementarily: in the past, the rational material (if one can so express it) with which people operated was relatively limited and could be surveyed. That is why one could disagree about many things, especially in the realm of world views, but nevertheless one could matter-of-factly presuppose—and did presuppose—that one understood and was understood when speaking or arguing with others. The conceptual material with which one operated and argued was relatively easy to survey. At least the theologians of all sides could presuppose that they were conversant with this material and with whatever problems could even be expressed, and that they could make themselves understood by their opponents. These opponents were dealing with the same very limited conceptual material and store of experience. Thus all sides presupposed a clear comprehension of what was said.

It does not matter whether this common self-understanding, the sameness and common clarity of the "language level," of the conceptual material, and of the culturally conditioned and mutually shared plausibilities really existed "objectively," or whether even in these earlier times controversies grew out of an unexamined difference in basic attitudes and presuppositions, etc. One did have this common self-understanding. Catholics, for instance, said that there were seven sacraments; Protestants rejected this but both sides presupposed that they understood themselves and their opponents and that they did not talk past each other. This common self-understanding, this homogeneity of language and thought levels, also shared by opponents, arose naturally out of an at least general unity of culture and out of the commonality of experiences shared in a limited and relatively small sphere (precisely one's own limited cultural circle).

The arguments were between brothers of the same family. Whatever could be known at all at the time could be known by a single individual—at least by a single educated and scholarly person. That the many, the uneducated, the common people did not know it was irrelevant. These masses of uneducated people were in any case condemned to keep their mouths shut in the disputes of the well educated and the scholars, and to subscribe to whatever views the political authorities and scholars of the time affirmed.

The world view of an earlier cultural era, insofar as it could be put into words at all, was either relatively clear and simple from the start, or became so again after short periods of crisis between intellectual eras. Such a world view was linked to a limited geographical and historical sphere and, for that reason alone, was already easy to grasp and relatively simple to deal with in controversies. It could be said that in the intellectual sphere one played with a limited number of balls, and could therefore play the game with virtuosity, even when it involved disagreements. At any one time, one could be convinced that one knew both one's own conviction and the conviction of the opposition which one rejected.

Today, this sketchily described situation of the confessional schisms of earlier times has changed significantly. It may even be possible to speak of a qualitative as well as quantitative upheaval, even though this change was historically slow at first, and even though it did not become evident to everyone until the present time.

Infinitely so much more is known today, that the single individual, even the very well educated and scholarly individual (as paradoxical as it may seem), is ever more impotent in comparison to the actual knowledge available in principle today. The number of books published is constantly increasing, and there is no one who can read them all. One can, of course, feed ever more data into ever larger computers, subject to recall. But despite all the syntheses that one can always strive for and even partly achieve repeatedly, which make it possible for a single individual to attain and control a previously uncontrollable amount of details, today's body of knowledge (even in computer memory banks) can no longer be surveyed or mastered by a single individual.

As an individual, one becomes ever more impotent; one has to depend more and more on the knowledge of others, which one can no longer assimilate or check oneself. It is precisely the most intelligent and truly educated who notice that, in every dimension of human life, they are in certain respects becoming more and more impotent and must increasingly depend on others. There are more and more experts on countless theoretical and practical matters who confront others the same way that, in earlier times, authorities and scholars confronted the impotent masses. But these experts understand each other very little, if at all, and thus form a choir of totally dissonant voices when they try to communicate their insights and precepts to others.

Everywhere in the world, the consensus in a society has the unfortunate tendency to move away from the unanimity of common, fundamental convictions, and to reduce itself to a consensus consisting solely of the selfsame materialistic presuppositions and needs. The ultimate reason for this is that the mass of what can actually be known has grown so terribly that it can no longer be synthesized in the simple fashion possible in earlier days.

The boundaries between the so-called educated and the uneducated have therefore become extremely unclear, in contrast to previous times. Today, there are no longer any either really educated or really ignorant people as such. Instead, all are in some sense educated and therefore simultaneously extremely ignorant in another sense. The universal scholar is extinct.

II

What does this primitive indication mean with regard to our *ecumenical question?*

First, the situation we have indicated is also a contributory factor to theology in all the churches. Here too one knows overwhelmingly more than previously—too much to prevent one single theologian, to say nothing of a single Christian, from becoming ever more impotent in comparison to this existing body of theological knowledge. The present exegete can no longer be a systematician as well, in the way required by systematics itself. The historian of dogma disparages—with a certain amount of justification—the systematic theologian, who plays with far fewer balls than New Testament theology and the history of doctrine could really offer him. Exegesis itself has become such a sublime science, using such a great variety of methods, that the individual exegete can boast of mastering only a small corner of his own field. Of course, there are still people in theology who pursue something like the function of a universal theological scholar. Perhaps they are even forced to strive for it if, for example, they are among the few in the Roman *Congregation of the Faith (Congregatio pro Doctrina et Fidei)* who must watch over and judge the orthodoxy of other theologians' doctrines.

Nevertheless, it becomes increasingly questionable whether, or to what extent, such a universal theological scholarship can be achieved by a single individual, particularly since today's technological advances in the scientific fields are of little use to the humanities. Theologians too know more and more, and for that very reason can understand each other less and less. The individual theologian cannot know for sure if he has understood the other theologian, because the latter can probably be understood correctly only if the former takes the latter's presuppositions into account, which, however, are just the ones the former can no longer find in his own head. Of course there are very many theologians and ecclesiastical officials who deny this existing situation in theology, who suppress it, and who still attempt to think and work in accordance with the situation of former times. They even have a certain fundamental right to do so, since one may not deny oneself the basic right to understand

29

and even to judge others as either correct or in error. But the present situation, which is qualitatively different from the earlier one, nevertheless exists and must be faced dispassionately and honestly.

Should I be more specific? I can be absorbed in the theology of a Rudolf Bultmann or a Karl Barth for ten years. But can I be sure I have understood them and judged them properly even then? I do not even study them that carefully, since I do not have the ten years to devote myself to them. Yet I cannot depend on the results of the real experts on theology either, because they do not agree with each other at all. I put all my strength into my study of Luther's theology and that of the Council of Trent. Do they ultimately contradict each other, or are they, in the final analysis, simply incommensurable but true? And did no one notice this earlier? How shall I generally proceed with regard to today's theology in the many churches, where truly real and truly great theology is at stake (on the whole, one can certainly give oneself credit for the ability to differentiate this—with a certain amount of risk—from run-of-the-mill theological babbling), in order to take cognizance of as much as possible and integrate it with my own? I really have no choice but to miss much in these theologies as something I cannot understand or assimilate, and to admire it as impenetrable (to me).

When I make a theological statement, I make every effort to be understood by others (at least within my church, to begin with), to respect a certain speech pattern of my church (and thus to discover, with a bit of good will, that what one wants to say can also be said by honoring this formality of language). But do I really and truly know that what I say is understood the way I "meant" it, that it says exactly what God's revelation said to us? It would not improve matters to merely repeat the approved ecclesiastical religious formulations. For I myself must interpret them correctly and express them in my own words. The history of truth does not stand still either, and so I have no choice but to try in my own words to express what these formulations mean and what they intend to say to us. But am I sure that my unavoidable interpretation is correct?

Naturally I am glad if the "official church" and the community of believers have no decisive and clear objection to my interpretation (that a few theologians do so anyway is not yet a valid condemnation of my theology). But does this prove that I am right and am not a heretic after all, particularly since some truly terrible heresies have been discovered long afterward and in retrospect (Jansen was dead already when Jansenism started its rampage)? I cannot expect any definitive responses (either affirming or rejecting), and even if there were some, I would not know with absolute certainty whether, even with all the obedience of faith I can muster, I had understood them correctly. It is not a simple or absolute certainty that authentic but not definitive declarations of the teaching office must always and in every sense be entirely correct. How then do I assure the harmony of my theology with true faith? Is it not necessary to have simple, handy rules?

In the final analysis, this situation may have been essentially the same in earlier times too. No one ever could see accurately into the head or heart of another, and every necessary and thus possible and meaningful dialogue among human beings is subject to this reservation. But this situation of uncertainty has nevertheless been unequivocally, terribly, and irrevocably intensified today. If all unity in faith nevertheless implies and presupposes an agreement on theology at all times, what happens to this situation of theologies and the incommensurability of their terminology, their "word games," the variety of plausibilities with which they start, etc.?

Because we theologians live and work in the one church of our confession, because we clearly participate in its life, because we are baptized, and because we specifically subject our theology to this church's confession as the norm of our own theology, we are convinced that we live in the same faith and thus possess a unity significant for salvation. Therefore we also have the eschatological hope that at some time the selfsameness of our faith will become clear, despite the present (partial) incommensurability of our theologies. All of us also still relate clearly and palpably (through baptism, confession, and Eucharist, together forming a dimension which transcends that of thought and speech) to Jesus as our Christ. But if unity of faith cannot be conceived of without a certain unity also of theology—which is obvious—how must this unity of faith be conceived of in the dimension of the church and its confession, if the situation of theology alluded to exists and is today irrevocable in light of the impossibility of synthesizing the elements of our intellectual and political circumstances? That is the question.

III

Before we consider directly the consequences to the essential ecumenical issue, which derives from the situation only alluded to above, one short *epistemological question* still has to be dealt with. If a person withholds an affirmative verdict regarding a true (certainly or possibly) proposition, he does not err. This truism applies not only when that person neither knows nor understands the proposition. He can also have been confronted with this proposition suddenly, more or less understand the sense of it, and still have morally justified reasons for withholding approval of it. These reasons do not necessarily need to lie in the inner factual doubtfulness or ambiguity of the proposition. They could be of another kind. For example, the proposition could be irrelevant to the existential circumstances of the individual concerned; the effort to test its claim of truth before approving it could be disproportionately great for the person concerned; the proposition, which in itself is correct, could be presented in a conceptualization inaccessible to that person, or in a field of understanding alien to him, and therefore could itself be hardly accessible. In cases like these, one will not be able to say that a certain proposition demands positive and clear approval from such a person, if for no other reason than that he should count on the truth of the proposition. If need be, he can respectfully let it drop without violating his moral duty to honor truth.

The following should be noted with regard to withholding agreement to a specific proposition which lays claim to truth: it is true—and is often and intensively put to use in Catholic religious practice—that the church itself is the guarantor, through its formal teaching authority, of the truth of the individual doctrines it presents.

But this does not mean that, first, every single Christian and Catholic who affirms this formal authority must therefore also bring it to bear, for emphatic and explicit affirmation, on every single proposition taught in this way. Even the Catholic who explicitly and positively affirms the formal authority of the church's teaching office will nevertheless frequently ignore individual teachings of this teaching office, or let them drop—even if he hears of them. He will, in that case, obviously not challenge or reject such a doctrine; one could also say that he has accepted it implicitly by basically affirming the teaching office. But even then it is possible for him to ignore that doctrine—to not affirm it positively and explicitly—and to do so for the reasons already indicated. Such a Catholic will fail to understand some aspects of the Council of Florence's definitive statements on the Trinity, for example, and will let them drop even if he does not challenge the formal authority of the church, and even though he may have heard of this conciliar doctrine.

Second, it must not be overlooked, in this connection, that the doctrine regarding the binding teaching authority of the church is not the first or most fundamental truth of the Christian faith in either the objective or subjective hierarchy of truths. That is proven by every normal Catholic fundamental theology, because the teaching authority of the church—including its responsibility and its limitations—is dealt with much later, only after very many fundamental themes regarding God, possibility and reality of revelation, Jesus Christ as mediator of divine revelation, the founding of the Church through Jesus Christ, etc.

Therefore it is entirely possible that a Catholic may live within the church, affirm in faith its fundamental doctrines, and yet still not have come to an explicit and positive affirmation of the church's formal teaching authority given to its officials in the way in which the church itself understands this teaching authority to be binding. Such a Catholic thus has the same relationship to the individual doctrine regarding the church's teaching authority as he has to other church doctrines which he does not positively reject but which he does not explicitly affirm either. Nevertheless, this Catholic (like other Christians who accept out of the mouth of their churches the gospel which through itself creates faith) naturally has a positive relationship to the church, and to that extent a (rudimentary) "churchly" faith. After all, he has in faith received the gospel, which contains the real fundamental truths, out of the mouth of his church. Thus in his faith he already recognizes a basic conviction that the church proclaims the truth of God and thus (to use Hans Küng's formulation) is maintained, on the whole, in the truth of God and of Christ. The result is still the same: not all truths taught by the church must be explicitly affirmed by the single individual.

What applies to the individual can obviously also apply to large groups of people. They too may have an existential lack of interest in certain propositions, for other legitimate reasons, even when they do not actively challenge these propositions, although the correctness of the propositions must be taken into account. Such groups, and therefore also individual churches, each have their own cultural and historical environment, in which they actualize their Christianity in part determined by that environment. They have their own religious history, in which they will discern a definite providence of God contributing to the development of their religious consciousness—with its positive developments and its limitations—despite all the ambiguity in this history, which will possibly have to be admitted.

It is certainly beyond argument that even in the same Catholic church there are large sociological groups and a variety of cultural circles, etc., which in their subjective hierarchy of truths have different principles and processes of selection, with regard both to what they grasp explicitly in their religious consciousness and piety and what does not really matter. One can ask, in a particular case, whether such differences in emphasis are praiseworthy or regrettable. But one will not be able to deny that these variations in actual religious structure exist within the Catholic church—not only among individuals but also among large groups (compared to each other). This observation is certainly confirmed by the teaching of the last council regarding the legitimate diversity in theology and piety between the churches of the East and of the West. In the actual religious consciousness of such groups and of the periods in the history of religion, it just is not true that this religious consciousness is structured in accordance with the *Systematic Index (Index Systematicus)* of Heinrich Denzinger,[17] or that it lacks nothing which is retained in the *Index*.

It seems evident that the churches (including the Catholic church) at least silently accept in their practice what has just been said. If a Christian is baptized, lives in his church, and to a certain extent participates in effectuating its life, that church considers this Christian a legitimate member of the church unit. It does not investigate more thoroughly which doctrines are accurately and explicitly present in the consciousness of this member, or how well he is informed about the whole dogma of this church. It does not ask whether he has a distinctly positive relation to specific propositions which it presents, and perhaps even proclaims, under certain historical circumstances of its life.

This church is satisfied if, on the one hand, this person makes it obvious in his church practice that he has a truly affirmative relation to the essential dogmas and to the ultimate fundamentals in the hierarchy of truths—even though it may be only a rather global and rudimentary one. On the other hand, this church is also satisfied if he does not raise explicit and decided objections, either inwardly or publicly, to doctrines which this church declares to be part of its objective essential faith.

The church knows that many religious and secular notions are contained in the personal consciousness of its members which do not really fit together. It knows that even when one of its members approvingly repeats and affirms a proposition it has formulated, it cannot be entirely certain that when he repeats that proposition the believer really thinks, understands, and concurs with what the church intends to say.

In view of the actually existing intellectual possibilities of the average person, it would be naive, when the average person clearly asserts he affirms a dogma of the church, to assume that he really affirms what this dogma intends to affirm in the sense of Scripture or the church's official proclamation. It would also be naive to assume, in every case, that the believer affirms a proposition and understands it in the official sense of the church just because he affirms the formal authority of the church in its official sense. That is precisely *not* the case, as was said before, because many Christians, including Catholics, frequently at least drop the formal authority of the church's teaching authority in its full sense, and yet are not troubled by the church's teaching office in the public life of the church. Nor should they be significantly troubled by it, because it would be exceeding their realistic potential to require more of them than they actually achieve. By participating in the life of the church, they prayerfully and hopefully grasp the fundamental truths of the gospel's message and let everything else slide, without raising the decisive protest of a conscience worried about its salvation.

All churches, including the Catholic church, are content with the fact that their members exist in a human, juridical, and liturgical unity as baptized and active members in the church. They thus help actualize the fundamental substance of the Christian confession (at least this may and must be presumed with regard to the church's public sphere in which it lives). But not every member is required to agree explicitly to every single proposition which the church itself considers part of its binding confession. This epistemological, in a sense minimalistic, tolerance is totally unavoidable, and is legitimate in the churches too.

IV

With this presupposition, and in view of today's intellectual-political situation contrasted to former times which was sketched above, it may now be said:

From the dogmatic viewpoint and with regard to the faith of the Church, a *unity of the still-separated mainline churches* would be conceivable if no church declares that a proposition considered by another church to be absolutely binding on itself is positively and absolutely irreconcilable with its own religious understanding. As long as discrepancies like *these* existed or still exist, there can of course be no thought of unity in faith among the churches.

But do discrepancies like *these* still exist today? One can question this. The theological consultations among theologians of the various confessions have in the last decades led to results which the church leaders have not yet taken sufficient notice of. It is certainly not true that the theologians of the various confessions and churches have already achieved a fruitful agreement on all dogmatic issues. These theologians can be seriously regarded as representatives of their own church's religious consciousness (which cannot be said of just anyone who pursues theology as a science of religion). But are there still many serious theologians today who would declare a proposition which a theologian of another confession held to be absolutely binding for his church to be downright irreconcilable with the faith the former holds decisive for *his* salvation?

The theologians of the various confessions are certainly not yet in clear and plain agreement on quite a few controversial theological issues. But the circumstances of their discussions have nevertheless changed radically in comparison to the time of the Reformation. Previously, each side confronted the other with positions which the other side declared to be objectively downright irreconcilable with the fundamental substance of Christianity. Consequently the other side was conceded only a possibility—if that—of salvation, since for some strange subjective reason it was held to be not really responsible for its false doctrine which, with good intentions, really could be recognized as false.

Today's theologians, with their perhaps not-quite-agreed-upon propositions, confront each other quite differently. On both sides, one counts on the fact that not only does a mysterious subjectivity excuse the other before God and before the truth of the gospel, but also that the propositions of both sides, when developed further and understood in a larger context, do not really contradict each other. However, one cannot yet determine clearly that they really do agree, even with such a broad interpretation, although we think that sufficient unity of faith among the churches can already be achieved in such a new situation.

The Protestant Christian would not need to make a doctrinal and definite agreement right now to many of the propositions that the Catholic regards as binding on the faith. But he does not need to reject them definitely either. As has become apparent from the historical development—and in light of the present intellectual-political situation—he cannot say that he can either affirm or ignore these specifically Catholic propositions only if he renounces what *he* justifiably counts a part of the substance of his own faith, as that would destroy faith. Nor does the withholding of judgment on such propositions mean that he must slowly move his religious consciousness toward *the* position *now* stated in these Catholic propositions. This Protestant Christian can most certainly assume that (hopefully) in the course of the further history of religious consciousness these Catholic propositions will obtain the kind of clarification and interpretation that will permit a definite agreement on his part (not yet possible today) without his having to feel duty-bound to reject them directly.

Conversely, in any unification of churches the Catholic ministerial office can be satisfied with the kind of religious position which mutually affirms the actual fundamental truths of Christian revelation. But for the sake of unity, there is no need to require a definite agreement to all the propositions which are conceived as objectively given along with divine revelation in the historical development of

37

the Roman Catholic church's religious consciousness. For their part, the Orthodox and Protestant churches can then be ready to reserve their judgment (on the basis of a content of *faith*) that specific Roman Catholic doctrines are downright incompatible with the revelation of God and the truth of the gospel, as was done at times of schism.

From the viewpoint of dogma, a unity of the churches is already possible today with this kind of epistemological tolerance. A consequence of this tolerance is that one does not cram radically contradictory but definite and explicit teachings together, and yet one makes room for the not-yet-agreed-upon but nevertheless acknowledged as agreed-upon. This sentence may seem daring, utopian, and perhaps even dogmatically controversial. But if one rejects the notion that a unification of the churches is simply impossible in today's intellectual-political circumstances—a notion surely prohibited by the fundamental convictions of Christianity and the Church—then one will have to admit that in today's intellectual climate no unity in faith is possible other than the one just proposed. Therefore it must be legitimate.

V

Let us imagine a more ideal and *more radical unity of faith* than what ecumenical Dialogues still consider the obvious goal, and then ask ourselves what this unity would actually look like if achieved in reality. Would not the theologians still quarrel, given today's intellectual-political situation? Would not those formulations of faith—which everyone had definitely agreed were generally binding—still be interpreted very differently according to the different limitations of understanding and with the different terminologies that would still exist and still be insurmountable in this pluralistic intellectual world? Actually, as a result of their restricted existential circumstances, would not individual believers and large groups of believers declare their lack of interest in certain doctrines? Would they not in fact silently withhold their clear agreement with these doctrines, a circumstance to be avoided in this more ideal unity of faith but acknowledged as legitimate in our own proposition?

One may say: either one declares the unity of faith to be an actually unachievable ideal to which one merely pays lip service, or one strives for a realistically conceivable unity of faith which one must then recognize as legitimate and attempt to make theologically comprehensible.

Once again, in different words: the unity of faith which actually exists in the Catholic church and must be legitimate is different from the unity of faith which one silently presupposes in theoretical ecclesiology to be self-evident. One considers the latter unity to be clear agreement (explicit, or at least implicit) to everything taught officially as binding dogma. But the unity of faith concretely realized within the Catholic church is also differentiated from the theoretically postulated unity of faith. And yet it is legitimate, and must be explicitly acknowledged as such. That is why *no more* must be required of the unity of faith in the one Church-to-be than the actually existing unity of faith in the Catholic church. But that unity must be clearly acknowledged as sufficient and legitimate.

Of course the Orthodox and the Protestant churches should also acknowledge this concept of the unity of faith as sufficient. But that should present no difficulties, since these churches at present already content themselves much more obviously with this unity of faith which we consider sufficient for the one Church-to-be. Actually, in this regard, the only requirement is that these other churches not reject out of hand an explicit doctrine of the Catholic church as being irreconcilable with the fundamental substance of their Christianity. The development of ecclesiastical consciousness in all the churches has progressed to such an extent that this is possible. Not, of course, in every one of these Christians or in every individual theologian in these churches. But one can assume that a majority of these Christians and theologians in the other churches will no longer pronounce an absolute anathema against such specifically Roman Catholic dogmas, and that therefore the leadership in these churches need not do so. Nor, under this assumption, does a clear affirmation of faith in these specifically Roman Catholic dogmas need to be exacted from these churches.

Thus a sufficient unity of faith can be established among all those who in faith comprehend the fundamental substance of Christianity in the confession to the triune God and Jesus as our Lord and Savior, and are baptized. The basic thesis is: in today's intellectual-political situation, no greater unity of faith is possible than the one proposed, and therefore it must be legitimate if the unity of the churches in faith is not to be abandoned despite all solemn declarations to the contrary.

When the present prefect of the Roman *Congregation of the Faith* declared that upon unification with Rome the Eastern churches may maintain the status of the doctrinal development they had at the time of their separation from Rome, this declaration definitely implies the thesis we present here. (Joseph Ratzinger made this declaration as a theologian and not as prefect, of course; but he did republish it at a time in which he was already prefect.) For there is no doubt that the development of dogma in the East had not yet progressed, in the year 1000, to the extent that a positive relationship with Rome could be expressed in conformity to the conceptualization of the First Vatican Council. An Eastern church connected to Rome in the unity of faith and in juridically arranged love certainly cannot reject the First Vatican Council's conceptualization as contrary to faith. But, according to Ratzinger, it need not really express this positive relationship to Rome in *the* conceptualization of the Latin West, which had attained a certain high point in the First Vatican Council. Thus, if the East may express the Western dogma regarding the universal jurisdictional primacy of the pope in different words, the practical and more juridical question of course comes up as to whether and to what extent this conception of the Roman pope's function—as it exists in a united Eastern church—also reveals the practical consequences which Latin Canon Law derives from this dogma and which it practices.

It is obvious that the actual canon law of the Western church, as formulated in both its earlier and its present fashion in the *Canon Law (Codex iuris canonici),* cannot simply be imposed on the Eastern church (or on the other churches and communities which desire unity with Rome). This law, in its actuality, cannot even be convincingly derived from the Western conceptualization of the Roman primacy. But even a concept of Roman primacy conceded by the Eastern church has certain juridical consequences. These questions, however, must be treated in other theses and their commentaries.

Of course, even if the proposed norm for the unity of faith is accepted in principle, many questions—even with regard to the unity of the Church as unity of faith—remain unresolved. If the theologians of the individual partner churches were to acknowledge and act according to this fundamental norm for the unity of the one Church—and thus did not reject any definitive dogma of the Roman church as contrary to the faith—these theologians would still have to strive to integrate positively the respective religious understandings of the other partner churches. (That is what the issue will be. Conversely, there should be very few difficulties, since there are practically no doctrines in the other churches which these churches teach as binding on the faith and as strictly binding on these churches and which are irreconcilable with Roman dogmas.) Models regarding correct relationships with each other already exist in the practice of individual theological schools which presuppose their own orthodoxy in the same church yet are different and strive to learn from each other.

One further problem would be: how should the appropriate officials of the individual churches and the Roman teaching office practically and concretely protect and defend this sufficient unity of faith of the unified churches conforming to this fundamental norm, since this unity of faith is certainly still being threatened? But this problem will be touched on in commentaries to other theses.

In our reflections on this Thesis II, the intellectual situation of today, with its existing new and unsurpassable pluralism in the thinking of the present and future, was taken into account from the very beginning. Therefore, in the light of a pluralism of thinking which can in no way be integrated into a higher synthesis, it would be totally unrealistic—at least at present and in future—to demand a larger and more tangible unity of faith. To be sure, without making explicit distinctions some of the reflections we presented can be considered independently of our analysis of today's situation. We do not need to investigate here whether these reflections could in themselves result in this Thesis II, without reference to the analysis of the situation. Presumably this is true. But then Thesis II would have fewer practical consequences than it does, since it was proposed and considered in light of the present intellectual-political situation from the very beginning.

THESIS III

In this one Church of Jesus Christ, composed of the uniting churches, there are regional partner churches which can, to a large extent, maintain their existing structures. These partner churches can also continue to exist in the same territory, since this is not impossible in the context of Catholic ecclesiology or the practice of the Roman church, as, for example, in Palestine.

For the sake of a realistic ecumenism which seriously intends to realize a unification of the mainline churches in the near future, Thesis III is probably crucial and at the same time really self-evident. It cannot be denied that, at least up to the time of Pius XI, the Roman Catholic church—perhaps not vis-à-vis the churches of the East, but certainly vis-à-vis the churches and ecclesiastical communities of the Reformation—had a notion that the unity of Christians, to be aspired to and to be realized, meant simply the return of the separated Christians to the Roman Catholic church. This would be achieved through a numerically large "conversion" of individual Christians (including the incumbent officials of these separated churches), with no change other than numerical growth anticipated for the Roman Catholic church itself. This notion is fundamentally refuted by the idea in the Roman Catholic church regarding unification with the Orthodox churches of the East, since this unification would grant to the Eastern churches their particularity in faith and liturgy, as well as their own canon law. It is also totally unrealistic with regard to the West.

I

It is simply inconceivable that the churches of the Reformation could ever be dissolved in such a way as to deliver their members, including their officials, to a Western Roman Catholic church without transforming that church. Not only is this a totally unrealistic expectation from the psychological and sociopolitical viewpoints and from the perspective of the unity and power these churches have achieved (each for itself). The demand that these churches surrender themselves is an illegitimate and unjust demand which simply may not be made by Rome in any way. With regard to the unity of the churches in the one Church, the Roman Catholic understanding of church is aware of a plurality of churches of differing structure and history, and in no way subscribes to the notion that the one Church consists solely of juridically and liturgically homogeneous segments. It would not even be desirable. Unification results in a more encompassing catholicity if it retains independent partner churches.

Vatican II, in *The Dogmatic Constitution of the Church* (*Lumen Gentium*) no. 13, emphasizes:

> Even in the ecclesiastic community, legitimate partner churches exist which benefit from their own traditions, without detriment to the primacy of the Chair of Peter. This Chair presides over the whole community of love, protects legitimate differences, and at the same time sees to it that the peculiarities do not damage this unity but indeed serve it instead. This is why, in the final analysis, the bonds of an intimate community of spiritual goods, of apostolic workers, and of temporal resources exist between the various segments of the church.[18]

In the *Decree on Ecumenism* (*Unitatis Redintegratio*, no. 14) the Council emphasizes that even before the separation between the Roman and the Eastern churches, "the churches of the East and of Europe each went their separate ways for centuries"; that "the inheritance handed down by the Apostles" was received in different forms and in different ways, and was therefore interpreted differently in these churches from the very beginning.[19]

Number 16 states, "From the very earliest times the churches of the East already had their own church orders which were sanctioned by the holy fathers and Synods, including Ecumenical Synods." It emphasizes that "a certain variety of customs and practices . . . in no way runs counter to the unity of the churches; indeed, it instead adds to its adornment and beauty, and contributes much to the accomplishment of its mission." There is the specific declaration "that the churches of the East, conscious of the necessary unity of the whole church, have the capability to rule themselves, in accordance with their own orders, in a manner most suitable to the spirituality of their believers and of greatest service to the salvation of their souls." It is conceded that this principle has not always been observed, but that it is a necessary precondition to the reestablishment of unity and must therefore be observed absolutely.[20]

Number 17 of the *Decree* describes this pluralism as a legitimate principle which refers to the theological proclamation of doctrine.

It is acknowledged that this whole spiritual and liturgical, disciplinary and theological, inheritance and its different traditions in the Eastern churches is a part of the full catholicity and apostolicity of the Church.[21] Therefore, with regard to unification of East and West, "no burdens should be imposed beyond the necessary things (Acts 15:28)" (no. 18).[22]

Thus the possibility, indeed the desirability, of a legitimate pluralism within the Church of particular churches with their own liturgy, their own constitution, and their own theology is an integral element of a Catholic concept of the true unity of the Church. A maximal homogenization of partner churches is not a Catholic ideal, even though the Council admits that, in actual practice, Rome frequently violated the legitimate autonomy of the Eastern churches within the unity of the whole Church.

It is true that the new Latin *Canon Law,* when it starts to deal with partner churches (*ecclesiae particulares*) in can. 368, immediately turns its attention solely to the diocese as such, and (as far as a thematic and explicit reflection is concerned) regards the larger partner churches as merely subsequent mergers of several dioceses. (Other smaller partner churches like a *praelatura territorialis,* an apostolic vicarage, a personal prelacy, etc., exist at the level of a single diocese at most to start with, and are therefore not relevant to our deliberations.) But the new Latin *Canon Law*'s concentration on the individual diocese is irrelevant to us.

First of all, the new Eastern church's canon law will certainly be aware of patriarchical churches, if only because in this law they are an essential factor for the appointment of individual bishops in the Eastern churches, since bishops are not simply appointed by the pope. Something like that is, from a dogmatic point of view, more significant than the ignoring of large partner churches encompassing many dioceses in the new Latin *Canon Law.* Moreover, the Western church of Rome is not really simply the sum of its individual dioceses either. The institution of Bishops' Convocations, concordats with nations which include several bishoprics, papal nuncios who are actually responsible not only for Rome's relations with nations but also for several dioceses together, etc., all demonstrate that larger partner churches exist objectively, and even juridically, in the Western church. They have their own unity and are distinguished from other large partner churches, but they are not identical with a single bishop's church.

But, even apart from canon law, there is the existence of large partner churches in the Latin church of the West which are in fact respected as such, though perhaps not sufficiently considered.

In Europe, there is in reality a French church and a German church, each with its own history and tradition, not to mention the problem of whether or how the dioceses of the German or the French church form an organizational unity juridically. Each of these churches has a common history of its own and therefore each has it own unity in the particularity of Christian life, of theology, and even to a certain extent in the field of official liturgy, in various styles of piety; each has its own history of relations with the governmental organization of the nation. Each of these churches also has a unity *as* church, a unity which is not simply commanded by Rome. It is not merely the sum of several dioceses combined for purely technical reasons. These churches are theological entities which Rome cannot ignore in its actual dealings with individual bishops and dioceses.

These facts have no less theological weight with regard to the essential legitimacy of the larger partner churches not indentical with individual dioceses, just because in other cases (for example, Denmark, Luxembourg, etc.) a large partner church of the type described does not clearly exist. In such cases, a national church is either identical with one or a few dioceses, or is merely the supplementary and external organizational unity of several dioceses for the sake of the unity of the governmental territory. Nevertheless, one can definitely speak of a church of Poland or Italy, even in a truly theological sense, particularly since the pope also claims the title "primate of Italy" besides the title "patriarch of the West."

The more the church in North America and the church in South America either achieve or have achieved their own particularity and identity on the basis of a national selfsame history, the more they will become large regional partner churches in the one Church. Their reality will have to be recognized, and has in fact already been recognized by Rome. For example, during his travels, the pope addressed the Latin American church as an independent entity.

There is undoubtedly an ecclesiological principle that the church is not constituted as merely the supplemental sum of individual dioceses. Instead, in accordance with history and contemporary reality, it is composed of large regional partner churches. Even though their size and particularity cannot be derived from an a priori principle of dogmatic ecclesiology, they must be experienced on the basis of both actual history and the present time. Therefore they do not signify a once and for all absolutely fixed entity. It seems obvious to us that the Third World churches are also growing into mainline churches and are developing their own particular individuality. Otherwise, any talk of the Church's acculturization in the different cultures would not be credible.

II

This principle is also applicable to the large churches formed by the Reformation of the sixteenth century. In the third chapter of its *Decree on Ecumenism,* the Council makes a justifiable distinction between the Eastern churches and the churches of the Reformation with regard to the greater or lesser distance of these churches from the Roman church. The council sees this difference particularly with reference to *doctrine.* The Commentary to Thesis II already dealt with that topic.

The issue in Thesis III is pluralism, with respect to the structure and discipline of individual partner churches. Therefore the thesis proposed here is: the ecclesiological principle of a legitimate pluralism of discipline and life in the individual partner churches can and should be applied not only to the Eastern churches (as the Council does explicitly) but also to the churches of the Reformation.

Of course, a unification of the churches is possible only if the Petrine office and its powers and functions are recognized sufficiently by all partner churches. This must be dealt with separately, in the commentary to other theses. But in this connection, it can already be noted that, with regard to unification with both the Eastern churches *and* the churches of the Reformation, this recognition of the particular functions of the papacy presents an ultimately similar problem. It cannot be presumed that the concrete form taken by the exercise of papal primacy, as it exists in the Latin church of the West, must also be the obvious form of the Roman primacy vis-à-vis the churches of the Reformation at the time of unification. Rome does not require this vis-à-vis the Eastern churches either, since it grants them their own canon law which has been and will probably continue to be distinguished from that of the Latin church.

When it comes to any unification, Rome can and must concede to the churches of the Reformation the same thing—from among all the preconditions—that it concedes to the churches of the East, on the basis of the ecclesiological principle of pluralism. Moreover, it should do so in the form of a concession binding on Rome. The churches of the Reformation must be considered in their present historical actuality. One cannot silently assume that the same salvation-historical and ecclesiastical situation exists today that existed at the beginning of the Reformation, in the sixteenth century, when Christians separated who had heretofore shared the same liturgy, the same discipline, the same theology, and the same church life.

Nor is it true—as perhaps a Catholic or a bishop whose church life has almost no actual contact with the life of the churches of the Reformation might assume—that these churches of the Reformation are distinguished from the Roman church only through deficiencies in doctrine, invalidity of ordination, etc. In their Christian life style, their liturgy, their theology, and in their relationship to secular realities, these churches have also clearly produced Christian and ecclesiastical realities which have a concrete form and liveliness not found so easily in the Roman Catholic church. Thus it must be admitted honestly and openly that, compared to these realities, the Roman Catholic church in fact exhibits deficiencies. At least, it pays tribute to the inescapably valid principle that nobody, in his particular (individual and collective) reality, can realize, all together and at once, everything that Christian grace and revelation has potentially given to both world and history.

The churches of the Reformation enlarge the one Church not only quantitatively but qualitatively if they unite with Rome. The treasure of all the churches together is not only quantitatively but qualitatively greater than the actual treasure that can be found in a single church, which also holds true for Rome. This admission was included in a draft (admittedly not actually said) of an address John Paul II gave in 1980, on the occasion of the Jubilee of the Augsburg Confession: "The Spirit of God has allowed us to recognize anew that as long as the church has not realized the fullness of its God-willed catholicity there are authentic elements of Catholicism existing outside its visible community." If that is so, then in any unification Rome must treat these churches of the Reformation as churches which, though heretofore separated, are nevertheless able to remain churches in a unification. Rome must not ask for their dissolution in order to achieve unity.

If, in their concrete actuality, the churches of the Reformation (we mean the large churches, not the sects which split away from these churches) would, without having to surrender themselves, integrate themselves into the one Church which would then include the existing Latin church as a partner church, and if all these uniting churches acknowledge the Petrine office to be valid for all and given to all, then the question certainly arises as to whether and how several partner churches can maintain themselves in the same territory, at least in larger parts of Europe and North America. The question can be fundamentally answered affirmatively, and can even be resolved with the coexistence of several partner churches in the same territory.

III

It must be said in essence that a Roman Catholic ecclesiology, both in theory and in practice, acknowledges that several partner churches of the same church can exist in the same territory. These partner churches differ in their episcopates, liturgies, specific canonical formulations, etc. For example, there are several Roman Catholic patriarchates in the same single territory of the Holy Land. In Germany and other countries, there are Ukranian exarchates in the territory of other dioceses of the Latin church. There may be some personal prelacies which, by their very nature, cannot have a territory bounded by that of other churches. Canon 372, par. 1 of the new *Canon Law* sets the "rule" that a diocese or dioceselike church is constituted through a specific territory and encompasses all believers living in that territory. But par. 2 of this canon explicitly states: several partner churches may be established in the same territory if, after a hearing with the Bishops' Conference concerned, the judgment of the highest authority of the church finds it to be useful and advisable.

These partner churches are distinguished by the rites of their believers. (According to the same par. 2, dioceses and prelacies may be established which are differentiated not through their rite but through other means. It is not clear what the "other reason (*alia ratio*)" is which distinguishes these partner churches in the same territory. Nor is it clear what is meant by the added statement that the rights of the local bishops must be protected.) In any case, it can be said, on the basis of both canon law doctrine and church practice, that several partner churches of the same church may exist in the same territory, and that this does not contradict the essence of the church.

If one should apply this principle to the problem of the unification of heretofore-separated churches, it cannot be denied that there is a significant difference between the cases to which this would now apply and the cases of partner churches of differing rite occupying the same territory to which it has been applied so far. For example—in the case of the unification here claimed to be possible, and also claimed to be the only realistically achievable one—if several large partner churches of the one Church were to live together it the same territory in Germany or North America, this would be a matter of churches which, in the number of their members, in the diversity of their structures and life, etc., differed significantly from the small partner churches in which this principle has so far been actually realized. But that does not mean that the same principle cannot also be applied to the new cases. There too it would be a matter of churches of differing "rite."

Nor, according to the doctrine of the new *Canon Law*, would it hold true that differences in rite are the only legitimation for a plurality of such partner churches in the same territory. And wherever a plurality of such partner churches exists in the same territory (for example, Palestine) a difference in liturgy is not the only difference they exhibit. Thus, in case of an ecumenical unification, it would be a matter of larger partner churches more important to the whole Church; but they too would fall within the scope of the essentially valid principle.

One must not overlook the fact that these partner churches already coexist peacefully and in a Christian manner before unification, and that by this very fact they are already proving that they can coexist peacefully after unification also. Today the relationship between the "separated" churches, in the same territory and in the same secular and national society, is no longer the same as it was in the old days after the Reformation. These separated churches no longer fight each other; they have fraternal ties and ties of friendship among themselves, even among their officials; they learn from each other; and they already cooperate in many areas. Thus it has really been proven already that they, different from each other and yet together, can also live together in the same church.

If, on the other hand, it is clear that it would be unrealistic to try to simply fuse them into a homogeneous uniform church, then this proposed principle can be applied: they can and should exist as distinct partner churches, of diverse rites and life styles and of distinct canon laws, as members of the one Church alongside each other and with each other in the same territory.

Of course the proclaimed principle cannot alone resolve many of the more practical problems. These distinct churches of differing "rite" cannot and should not simply live alongside each other with indifference. They should not form a unity solely through their common relationship to Rome; they should have lively interchanges with each other. We shall have to deal with pulpit and altar fellowship specifically at a later time.

It is self-evident that there must be fraternal exchanges and intensive cooperation among the theologians of these partner churches, even though this in no way requires the fusion of the institutional and organizational representatives of the theologies of these distinct churches. Agreements (including juridical and organizational) must certainly be made concerning many aspects of these churches' actual life, so that respect, exchange, and cooperation of these churches is ensured. Reasonable and practical regulations must be set for the transfer from one partner church to another, similar to the regulations already established for a change of rite in today's Roman Catholic church. A more detailed description of what pulpit and altar fellowship means, and what it does not mean in specific cases, must be produced. Many specific problems, which we cannot list here, must be resolved. How, for example, do these churches live together and yet differ on the issues of the celibacy of ordained priests, of the number of "commanded" Sundays and festivals, and of taxation of members? These and countless other questions should be answered, and practical solutions found.

The difficulty of finding solutions to these questions is no reason to renounce church unity. Even with lasting recognition of the validity of diversity among these churches, the solution to these problems will nevertheless require that all sides give up a certain number of old familiar customs, so as to make possible not just coexistence with tolerance and much indifference but a true unity of these partner churches in truly loving recognition of their differences.

This does not yet refer to the mutual recognition of the ministerial offices and their sacramental and legal powers, which will be dealt with separately. Rather, it refers to other mutual "concessions" which would make the coexistence of the partner churches in unity and diversity as fruitful to all as possible, and which would enable their service to the world.

One should, of course, examine in detail which churches and church communities would really qualify for unification in accordance with Thesis III. In Germany, for instance, this would be the large Protestant territorial churches individually, or the Evangelical Church of Germany (EKD) as a whole, but not the smaller church groups or sects, even if these declared their basic desire for unity. Smaller religious communities, even if they desired unity, could probably not really fit into the adjusted landscape of the Church in unity and diversity, because they are too small and they would contribute too little historical substance with regard to Christian experience and Christian life. Above all, if one honored Thesis II, even their continued existence with the unity of faith in the one Church would not be possible, because the formal principle of their existence as such would be in clear contradiction to the essence of the common faith. But these reflections may be superfluous, since these Christian communities will reject such unity on their own.

IV

In connection with Thesis III, the question can well be asked: what *authority* in the other large Christian churches seeking to become integrated into the one Church as partner churches is really competent to agree to the presuppositions for unity set forth in this thesis and to declare them valid? It is obvious that for the Roman

Catholic side it is the pope, in conjunction with all the bishops of the nations concerned, who is competent. It is also illuminating that, based on the Roman Catholic church's self-understanding, such a decision on the part of the pope and the bishops is essentially binding on the Catholics of this church. One can say something similar about the Orthodox churches.

But the problem becomes more difficult with regard to the large churches of the Reformation. They do indeed have their ecclesiastic leadership—bishops, presidents, etc.—including the other members of their church governing bodies who participate in the decision-making process. With regard to our topic, it is not really important for the Roman Catholic church to know exactly how, juridically or practically, the governing body of a Protestant church arrives at its agreement to church unity.

Nevertheless, on the basis of the present Protestant understanding of Church, it is not easy to answer the question whether and to what extent the remaining members of such a church (ordained pastors and actual congregations) actually would affirm such a decision of their ecclesiastical leadership and carry it out. (The ineffectiveness of the agreement between Rome and the East at the Council of Florence is a warning not to overlook such difficulties.) Insofar as such a unification is still a matter of faith rather than of merely human organization, one could ask whether an officially decided-upon unification would not be rejected by Protestant Christians. Their reason would be that unification runs counter to their religious conscience and that they had from the very beginning denied their governing bodies the power to make binding decisions in matters affecting the faith.

With regard to this difficulty and danger, one will certainly be able to say that the ecclesiastical leaders of the churches of the Reformation will make sufficiently sure of the support of the majority of their members before making the decision. One will have to admit soberly that, in today's intellectual-pluralistic society, a *unanimous* affirmation of a decision to unity cannot be expected. Nor should it be forced on anyone. But it is presupposed, and it is necessary in order to achieve church unity.

Based on Thesis II, one may well say, with regard to such unification, that one cannot expect the *clear* agreement of many Protestant

Christians to this unification as a matter not merely of organization but a matter demanded by faith. But this agreement need not be demanded if Thesis II is valid and if these Protestant Christians do not clearly reject this unity as being contrary to faith on the basis of their conscience. Most of them will not do that, precisely because of their "liberal" way of thinking; in matters of faith they concentrate solely on the fundamental convictions of Christianity and count the rest as adiaphora.

There will be quite a few practical difficulties in this matter, even if one assumes that what was said above is correct.

In comparison to earlier times, the directly accessible and familiar life of the Protestant congregations integrated into the unity of the one Church will exhibit far fewer changes in compliance with Thesis III than one would have to expect if Thesis III were not clearly honored. But some changes are unavoidable, because of the respect for unity and a legitimate, albeit carefully delimited, claim to leadership on the part of Rome even vis-à-vis these congregations. These changes could in fact arouse some protest in these congregations.

However, even if one recognizes a significant difference in parish life between Catholic and Protestant congregations, with respect to ecclesiastical leadership the average congregation in the Protestant churches in fact usually practices the kind of obedience to their church leaders that is customary in the Roman Catholic church. Therefore one should not overestimate the danger of a rebellion "at the grass roots" against their ecclesiastical leaders' decisions regarding unification. On the basis of their theological expertise and their religious conscience, the representatives of this ecclesiastical leadership can decide in favor of church unity, and can also work with sufficient zeal among the church members to gain their understanding for this decision. As always the presupposition is, of course, that one's conscience comprehends this unity as a truly binding commandment of Christ, and that one is prepared to dare something, the good results of which cannot be foreseen with absolute certainty.

V

A greater similarity in *sacramental life* must be added to these concrete adaptations still to be carried out among the individual partner churches. There is no great difficulty in uniting the Roman church and the Eastern church on this issue, since the Orthodox churches know the seven sacraments in essentially the same way as they are taught and lived in the Roman church.

Difficulties on this matter increase with regard to unification with the churches of the Reformation, since, at least at first glance, they acknowledge only two of the seven sacraments as they exist in the Roman church. With regard to the ultimate essence of the sacraments, there should be no difficulties, if Thesis II is taken into account.

All the churches can regard the sacrament in general as the manifest Word of their Lord. With binding force the church speaks this word, as the enduring presence of God's victorious mercy in the world, to the real and particular circumstances of a human being. All the large churches of the Reformation have an understanding of this manifest Word of grace derived from Christ (which is identical with what the Catholic church calls *opus operatum*). Difficulties arise with regard to the number of such sacraments. Even when taking Thesis II into account, one will have to say that in future the partner churches of the Reformation will essentially have to acknowledge and observe the remaining sacraments in principle, even though the actual practice of them need not be identical with that of the existing Roman church. Something like this appears to be quite feasible.

First of all, the churches of the Reformation will have to acquire— if they have not already done so—a more or less new understanding of the origins of Christ's sacraments, on the basis of the new findings from the history of doctrine. This kind of understanding was not possible at the time of the Reformation. At least baptism (if we disregard the Lord's Supper) can no longer be thought of in quite so simple and undifferentiated a way as "instituted" by Jesus, as the Reformation did when it used this to distinguish baptism from the remaining Roman sacraments. Instead, baptism may be thought of as coming from Jesus (in the manner of: "established") which is really how one should think of it everywhere today (namely, as stemming from the power of the gospel's Word and from the essence of the Church, which really already exists through cross and Resurrection). In that case any insistence on any literal, tangible words of institution from Jesus with respect to sacraments would really be obsolete. It would then be easy to see that the manifested Word of

Jesus on the lips of the Church (called sacrament) exists in forms other than the Word of baptism and of the Lord's Supper, and is called sacrament. This would hold true, particularly in the sense of the Council of Trent, even if these other ways in which the Church effectively promises to human beings the Word of grace beyond baptism and the Lord's Supper not only may, but should be considered clearly distinct from the Word of grace of baptism and of the Lord's Supper.

In accordance with the Augsburg Confession (XI, XII, XXV),[23] the word of forgiveness to terrified consciences can also definitely be understood as sacrament, especially since such a word of forgiveness exists in the Lutheran churches. With regard to the frequency of the sacrament of penance, it can be conceded by the Protestants that, in cases of a sin which, according to Paul, "excludes from the kingdom of God," this word of forgiveness from the Church is basically required.

As far as the sacramentality of marriage is concerned, at least one difficulty for Church practice would be cleared away if the churches, in the style of today's Roman church, would in the united Church in essence relinquish the particular statute dating from the Reformation, according to which a wedding takes place in front of the church. This is quite possible according to Roman theology and marital canon law. Under this condition, these churches could relinquish an explicit official ecclesiastical doctrine regarding the sacramentality of marriage, in conformity with Thesis II. The exact interpretation of what is in fact a sacrament according to Roman Catholic understanding could then remain an open question in these partner churches. Marriage is a holy reality before God and conscience, according to the teaching of Jesus and Paul. That is also what it is, in any case, to a believing Christian of the Reformation churches.

On the issue of "confirmation," it should not in any way be overlooked that even in a Roman Catholic understanding of the history of doctrine it can be understood as a (legitimate) offshoot within the total initiation into Christianity. From the dogmatic viewpoint, it can be dispensed in a great variety of ways (laying on of hands, anointing) and it may be done either in direct connection with baptism or separately. If one considers all of this and also clearly understands the real fundamental essence of a sacrament—which cannot be revealed at all merely through explicit reflections on sacramentality—then at the time of unity one can conceive of a confirmation even in the Reformation churches which would occur either simply in connection with baptism or, for example, at a (liturgically well conducted) confirmation service in the Protestant churches.

As for extreme unction—which can certainly appeal to New Testament practice—one should not overlook how variously the Roman Catholic church has interpreted extreme unction in both theory and practice. Moreover, it must be clearly seen that, with regard to the frequency of extreme unction, it has had a very checkered history in the Roman Catholic church. If the partner churches stemming from the Reformation would make a discreet offer to administer such unction as spiritual assistance to the sick, which certainly is part of the pastoral practice in these churches, by referring to the New Testament era, this would probably present no insurmountable difficulties to Protestant pastoral practice. In accordance with Thesis II, the exact theological meaning of such a meaningful rite could remain open; such a practice would also satisfy the dogmatic doctrine regarding extreme unction in the Roman Catholic church.

Ordination will be dealt with in greater detail in the Commentary to Thesis VII.

THESIS IVa

All partner churches acknowledge the meaning and right of the Petrine service of the Roman pope to be the concrete guarantor of the unity of the Church in truth and love.

I

To postulate such a thesis as presupposition for the unity of faith and Church unity among the Christian churches would have appeared unimaginable until a few years ago. It would have been regarded as pure illusion. The rejection of the papacy, the anti-Roman effect, the "away from Rome," the cry "no popery," all seemed to be an affiliation overcoming all other differences of non–Roman Catholic churches and Christians.

The papacy and its accompanying claims in the church, but also the pope's politics—both domestic and foreign—seemed to be the real cause of the separation of the churches of the East and the West. This separation had been sealed in 1054 by mutual excommunication, and since then created a condition of schism associated with growing alienation. The separation of the European church into diverse confessions or "religious parties" began when the Reformation churches rejected the pope and his office of supreme leadership and of determinative teaching which claimed to be binding.

They clothed this rejection in the most extreme formula coined by Luther, that the pope was the antichrist, and that the papacy had been instituted by the devil, because the pope had refused to listen to the Reformation message and had resisted it. In the Smalcald Articles, Luther said: the Church could never be governed and preserved better than if we all lived under the one Christ, and the bishops were all equal in rank; but the pope had raised himself above the other bishops; this showed that he was the true antichrist, who had set himself above Christ and refused to leave Christians without his authority;[24] the Church had become the supreme and highest monarchy under the pope.[25]

For his part the pope rejected, as conflicting with the tradition of the church, the fundamental truths of the Reformation—the so-called material principle of justification by faith alone without works; and the formal principle of Scripture alone, which is its own interpreter and needs no papal teaching office. According to Luther, even pope and council could err. The papacy was also rejected in large measure because the Word of God was being manipulated, since the church identified itself with revelation itself. The separation of the European churches in the sixteenth century was a great deal more significant than that between the Eastern and Western churches, for it concerned faith itself, in fact its very center.

The time of the Counter-Reformation and of the Catholic Restoration which followed only sharpened the antagonism between the confessions, which was disclosed precisely in face of the papacy. The Catholic church of the West sought to define itself through the "Roman," that is, through the fact that the increasingly prominent papacy became the specific and outstanding symbol of the church itself. That is how the term "papal church" originated. The development led Catholic apologetics to make the "Romanitas" into the characteristic and the symbol of the church which included all others; if it was missing, there could be no talk of the true and single Church of Jesus Christ.

The nineteenth century, which saw the end of the imperial church and which imposed a heavy and humiliating fate on the popes, gave rise to a pronounced papalism under the sign of the Restoration. Indeed, a veritable papal cult started to bloom, which frequently approached tastelessness and blasphemy.[26] These tendencies were combined with a pronounced defensiveness on the part of the Catholic church against the spirit, hostile to the faith, of the age—the culmination of the modern era. This defensiveness dominated the entire century.

One thought that the roots of this modern era could be traced back primarily to the Reformation, besides other circumstances. It was defined and thus distorted as "so-called" Reformation—one should rather speak of rebellion or revolution—and was regarded as one of the sources of modern corrupt subjectivism and confusing relativism.

The Roman Catholic church thought there was only *one* answer to give in response—the reinforcement of the unity of the church on all sides, as well as the comprehensive demonstration of what is "objective." The best way to ensure both was thought to be through the

60

objectivation of faith in the form of dogma and doctrine, and through the most comprehensive designation possible of the highest office in the church, the "summespiscopate" of the Roman bishop, the pope. The supreme and full jurisdiction over the whole church and the individual churches, which united in him, was intended to be the surety to guarantee unity through the orientation to the center and through the greatest uniformity possible in all aspects of church life. The dogmatic definition formulated at Vatican I in 1869/70 regarding the primacy of the pope as universal jurisdictional primacy and, related to this, the definition of the infallibility of his teaching office ex cathedra, were intended to articulate what the supreme office in the church is to signify and effect as center of unity.

The Vatican I *First Dogmatic Constitution on the Church (Constitutio Dogmatica I "Pastor aeternus" de Ecclesia Christi)* declares that Christ, "the eternal shepherd and bishop of our souls," appointed Peter as abiding principle which unites bishops and priests, and as visible foundation; that the Petrine primacy had been founded by Christ; and that Peter had received jurisdictional primacy personally and directly from Jesus. John 1:42, Matt, 16:16ff., John 21:15 were referred to as documentation, but not Luke 22:32. Then the *Constitution* mentions "perpetuity *(perpetuitas)*," the uninterrupted continuity of the Petrine primacy in the Roman popes. This proof is documented with three historical witnesses: Leo I, Irenaeus, and Ambrose.[27] Even disregarding their relatively late date, however, these witnesses are in no way as clear within their historical context as the conciliar declaration claims they are.

The Vatican I definition of the primacy of the pope as of "divine law *(ius divinum)*" was made at the very moment that saw the end of the papal territory and thus the end of the pope's political power. There had been no lack of voices beforehand desiring to make a dogma out of the necessity of the papal territory for the realization and exercise of the papacy. Theologians who warned against this, like Ignaz Döllinger and John H. Newman, were accused of disloyalty to the church. When the papal territory could no longer be maintained, there was increased pressure to emphasize the moral authority and position of primacy of the pope within the church, and to make it a declaration binding on faith.

After the council, when Bismarck and Gladstone compared the Roman church to an absolute monarchy "worse than any form of government in the world" which raised doubts about the loyalty of citizens, their views were explicitly rejected, expecially in a noteworthy declaration by German bishops in 1875[28] which was welcomed by Pope Pius IX. But the comparison remained an effective image, particularly since monarchy was considered to be the best system of government. Why should it not be applicable to the church, the perfect society?

One could supply ample evidence to prove how much these decisions of Vatican I regarding the primacy and teaching office of the pope have burdened the relationship to other confessions almost to the present day. The Old Catholic church was founded because it rejected Vatican I. "They created a new church" (Döllinger). One might mention Karl Barth's statement in his *Church Dogmatics* about "the Vatican sacrilege"; about the church of insolence and of disobedience to the Word of God, over which the Catholic teaching office—the teaching office of the pope uppermost—rules arrogantly and judgmentally. One might also mention Peter Brunner's words, as late as 1967, that the dogmas of Vatican I disclosed to the full extent that the fundamental decision of the Reformation and its exclusive orientation to the Word of God is irreconcilable with the Roman church's understanding of teaching office. This opinion was reinforced when Pius XII decreed in 1950 that the bodily assumption of Mary into heavenly glory was to be believed as divine revelation.[29]

This proves to be even more correct since Vatican II repeated the formulations of Vatican I, including the misleadingness regarding the declaration that the ex cathedra decisions of the Roman bishop are "irreformable" "out of himself (*ex sese*)," not on the basis of the church's agreement. It has already been pointed out frequently that the texts of Vatican II—which was asked to supplement Vatican I and intended to do so—have more references to the pope, more often, than Vatican I. The "*nota praevia* (advance notice)" which was communicated to the council fathers in connection with the church Constitution, *Lumen Gentium*, through the general secretary, on behalf of a "higher authority," contains the sentence which is not contained with equal harshness and misleadingness in Vatican I: "The pope, as supreme shepherd of the church, can exercise his power at any time he sees fit, as is demanded by virtue of his office" (no. 4).[30]

So that is where it stands: the issue of the papacy is a still unresolved ecumenical problem. It stands between the Roman Catholic, Orthodox, Anglican, and Reformation churches, not to mention the so-called free churches.[31]

Even theologians who no longer discern a church-dividing quality in other previously controversial issues—and indeed see in them a possibility for reconciled diversity—so far find the issue of the papacy a seemingly uncrossable border barring the way to a unity of the Church in faith and in truth. They thus repeat a statement of Pope Paul VI who declared, when he visited the World Council of Churches in Geneva, "I am Peter. The office of Peter, created for the unity of the Church, had become its greatest obstacle."

II

Then how is it possible to nevertheless set up the thesis that all churches can acknowledge the meaning and right of the Petrine service of the Roman pope to be the concrete guarantor of the unity of the Church in truth and love?

The following reasons are probably decisive:

(a) The papacy is regarded as *Petrine service* and as Petrine office—and that is more than just a superficial change. It points to the biblical evidence regarding the person of Simon Peter. The exegetical work in all confessions has been directing its attention to it and has achieved a surprising convergence; all the gospels in the New Testament contain a definite Petrine tradition which awards a leadership role to this apostle. The mere naming of Simon as "Peter," which has supplanted the original name, "Simon," is not the distinguishing of a particular character trait. Rather, it is the indication of a specific function within the college of the Twelve and the messianic congregation addressed by Jesus: Peter is to be the rock, that is, its foundation and its cohesion. This function is further modified through the image of the power of the keys transferred to Peter, with which a kind of discretionary authority is expressed, as well as an indication of the right to judge doctrine. The words about binding and loosing addressed to Peter—but also to the twelve—denote a juridical competence in matters of leadership and of order in a community, a power to admit or to exclude.

The service of Peter is further defined by the admonition to strengthen the brothers in faith (Luke 22) and to tend the flock of Jesus (John 21). Peter was the spokesman for the Twelve when they confessed the Messiah; the Risen One appeared first to him (1 Cor. 15); he played a leading and decisive role at the so-called apostolic council (Acts 15); he was the first leader of the original congregation in Jerusalem; and, according to the testimony of the history of the apostles, he accepted the first Gentile, the centurion Cornelius, into the community of the early church. According to ancient tradition, Peter went to Rome and died a martyr's death. His temporary controversy with Paul (Gal. 2:11) is not a refutation but a confirmation of Peter's special status.[32]

All of this bespeaks a special service, a specific function, a leadership role. All of this expresses a certain primacy for Peter, although it would be anachronistic to define it in the same dimensions that Vatican I did in its dogma of universal jurisdictional primacy.

According to the New Testament, this Peter image is augmented by the fact that Jesus called Peter not only rock but also stumbling block (*scandalum*); that he failed and confessed his failure; that he had to be pulled out of the water when he was sinking (Matt. 14:28–31); that he had to be rebuked in the name of the gospel, and that he accepted the rebuke without striking back; that he did not always occupy the leadership position in the first congregation and yet remained the first. That is what dialectic does to the image of Peter.

Certainly the testimony given above applies first of all to the first apostle called by Jesus, Simon Peter. Nothing is said specifically about a *succession* in this service. But the following reflection does not contradict the biblical evidence; the functions and services assigned to Peter, including the function of the rock of the Church of Jesus, cannot be restricted to the person of Peter, if the church is to remain in history. These facts must also be taken into consideration with regard to the permanence and continuation of the apostolic services and of the apostolic office, especially with regard to the office of proclamation—and thus with regard to the problem of the apostolic succession as a whole. This permanence in the case of the

Petrine service is expressed in Matt. 16:17–19, where the reference is not so much to a single and then completed cornerstone laying as to a *founding function*.[33] This function, as function and service to a community, can be perceived only through a person who assumes these original functions in a permanent community of the church.

If one asserts that the Petrine tradition of the New Testament, especially Matt. 16:17–19, appertains to a later time, one should be able to explain why it happened. Moreover, why should one be interested in such an office and service, if it does not correspond to a true reality and to an important position in the life of the Church?

It is undoubtedly a long way from the Petrine service, as described in the New Testament, to the papacy in its historical form and prominence, particularly in its representation as coined by Vatican I. A combination of circumstances, among them the fact that Rome was the capital of the Roman Empire, played a part along the way. But the significance of the fact that the papacy today conceives itself to be explicitly Petrine service and Petrine office cannot be rated highly enough. Thus the papacy seeks to gain its fundamental orientation in the biblical source, which has, at the same time, a critical function vis-à-vis later history and tradition.

It is not proof but a rather important indication that the very early church of Rome and its leader (*First Epistle of Clement*), already occupied a special position (a "more preferential rank (*potior principalitas*)," Irenaeus) and performed a prominent and recognized service to the unity of the Church. A particular loyalty to the apostolic heritage was ascribed to the church of Rome at the time of the *Gnosis*. Rome functioned as the court of orientation, mediation, and appeals in the early church; eucharistic fellowship with Rome meant eucharistic fellowship with all the churches. Its importance is only underlined by the fact that the Apostles' Creed as baptismal creed originated in Rome, and that the quarrel over the validity of baptism performed by heretics (*Ketzertaufstreit*), as well as the question of the biblical canon, were decided in Rome.

To be sure, popes have based their claim to the primacy of their office on the Petrine texts of the New Testament only since the third century. Leo the Great, who assumed the title "vicar of Peter (*Vicariis Petri*)" did so most emphatically. Gregory the Great used the title "servant of the servants of God (*Servus servorum Dei*)" to describe that claim. On the other hand, no city but Rome laid claim to being the seat of the successors to the office and service of Peter.[34]

It would go too far to see merely an organic development in everything that was said about the function and service of Peter in the New Testament. On the other hand, one can agree with W. de Vries about points of departure which permit the statement "the development which actually occurred at least does not conflict with the New Testament."[35] It is therefore legitimate to ask "whether and in what manner later experiences and developments can be substantiated by referring back to the New Testament and to ancient tradition. Thus the theological question is posed anew in less rigid terms vis-à-vis the existing Apologetics."[36]

Measured against the sometimes prevailing maximal notions of the Catholic side, this may be a relatively modest report about the papacy. But it is honest, and it accords with historical developments. Moreover, it presents the indispensable conditions for starting an ecumenical dialogue regarding a possible Petrine service in the one Church-to-be.

(b) A second reason for renewed ecumenical attention to a Petrine service in the Church can be seen in the following fact: Luther repeatedly declared—the last time as late as 1531—that he would accept the pope and his leadership office; indeed he would "uphold him and kiss his feet" if only the pope would accept "his" gospel regarding the justification of human beings, or if he would at least tolerate it. But that did not happen in a way available to Luther at the time.

One can go to ask what happens, however, if, according to the opinion of most Protestant and Catholic theologians today, the doctrine of justification, "the article on which the Church stands and falls" has lost the quality of being church-dividing? What happens if, in the sense of reconciled diversity, it holds a legitimate position? Should this not lead to a review and reconsideration of the image of the pope and of the form of the papacy, even if the consensus of the theologians regarding this issue has not yet been officially accepted by the churches?

But this process is underway; it will not take an opposing turn, nor will it once again take on a church-dividing quality. Furthermore, a relatively great openness exists in the Protestant view regarding the full recognition of the divinely instituted ministerial office in the church, which it sees as the single office. "Precisely because Lutheran thought is open, free, and unprejudiced on questions of office, with regard to its concrete formation, it can be flexible on the question of a universal office."[37]

(c) The following fact is to be seen as the decisive reason for putting the issue of the Petrine service in the papacy in the sense of the proposed thesis: the time of interconfessional polemics is gone. So is the time of controversies focused solely on substantive differences. And so is the time of using simple confessional methods of comparison whereby one's own historically actualized confessional viewpoint was made the decisive criterion for judging the other. All this is gone in favor of an ecumenical consciousness which determines all churches, and which exists in antecedently given unity in the fundamental truths of faith. Tied to this is the effort to strive for the community of the churches in faith, in truth, and in love, and, in full recognition of God's gracious freedom in history, to do everything possible to overcome the separation.

People—Christians—caused the separation. What was done historically cannot be undone, but history—as the place of human freedom and as stage of the new and frequently surprising—can be changed by people. To do so is duty when what has happened historically and what has become historical is proven to be contrary to the source and also proves to be something that should not be.

Present ecumenical consciousness caused the step from "anathema to dialogue" to be taken and to be applied also, and precisely, to the papacy and the Petrine office.

On the Roman Catholic side, this consciousness was effected primarily through Vatican II and its intentionally ecumenical goals.

Furthermore, it must be said that although Vatican II repeated without restrictions the Vatican I doctrine of primacy, it did set this issue in a larger context and thus drew it out of its isolation. It prefaced the doctrine with a reflection on the Church as sacrament and mystery of unity, and as people of God to whom all offices in the Church are assigned. This was followed by a detailed treatment of the bishop's office and the College of Bishops—the first of whom is the pope, who cannot be described in his functions without the College of Bishops. There was, finally, an intimation of the significance of the local churches as well as the laity in matters of faith.

III

Steps along the way to an approach of the partner churches to a Petrine office as concrete guarantor of the unity of the Church in truth and love.

(a) The reconciliation of the churches of East and West is a decisive event. In December 1965, Paul VI ceremoniously revoked the bull of excommunication which had been sent out in 1054 against the then-patriarch of Constantinople, Michael Cerularius. The bull was to "be erased from memory and removed from the center of the church." At the same hour of the same day, Patriarch Athenagoras "submitted to forgetfulness" the ban which Michael Cerularius had imposed on the Roman cardinal Humbert von Silva Candida against the Latins; a delegation of the Roman Catholic church was present at the ceremony.

A joint declaration of the Roman Catholic church and the Orthodox church of Constantinople was read in St. Peter's. The declaration stated that from then on nothing could hinder the fraternal rapprochement of the two churches; that both churches represented the desire of all Christians for unity; that both churches regretted the old insults and injurious actions; that both churches were aware that this declaration had not yet overcome both old and new oppositions, but that, with further examination of conscience and with good will, they could be completely rectified; that the dialogue to achieve this end had been established on a new basis of trust, for hearts had been purified by these events.

Patriarch Athenagoras captured the sense of the event with the words, "The seventh of December signifies a light which dissipates the darkness that has clouded a period of the Church's history, now past; this light illumines the present and future path of the church."[38]

According to Ratzinger, forgetting past events should be followed by a new remembering, which would work on the healing of memory and which would lead from love (*agapē*) as ecclesial reality to eucharistic love (*agapē*).[39] This is already possible and desirable under certain conditions, and has been made clear in the *Decree on Ecumenism (Unitatis Redintegratio,* no. 15).[40]

From the ecumenical viewpoints in general, one cannot point out forcibly enough the fact that the Roman Catholic church is offering eucharistic fellowship to the Orthodox church even though there is no universal unity in faith between the two churches. The Orthodox church is not accepting the Vatican I dogmas regarding the jurisdictional primacy and infallibility of the pope. This sheds some light on the double assertion, itself not communicated very clearly, "The Eucharist requires and *furthers* the unity of the Church." Obviously that also says that the (jointly celebrated) Eucharist is also a reason for, not just a consequence of, Church unity.

What conclusions can therefore be drawn from this with regard to a eucharistic fellowship with the churches of the Reformation? What are the consequences of the fact that, as has been said, there are no longer any church-dividing obstacles between them and the Roman Catholic church, other than the issue of the papacy? What results from the fact that precisely this church-dividing issue does not prevent a eucharistic fellowship with the Orthodox church? This state of affairs cannot be limited to the relationship between the Orthodox and the Roman Catholic churches. It opens up whole new ecumenical means and possibilities that have not yet been sufficiently thought through as to their consequences and import.

Ten years after the revocation of the mutual excommunication, during a worship service dedicated to that event, Pope Paul VI gave an impressive sign which was observed by all of Christendom. He fell on his knees before Metropolitan Meliton, the ambassador of the ecumenical patriarch of Constantinople, and kissed his feet. The significance of this gesture can be made clear when one remembers that "prostration (*proskynese*)" was for a long time reserved for the pope alone. Thus the gesture was interpreted to mean that if the pope requires this "submission" of himself he is going to the very limits of self-denial and is demonstrating by these radical means how much unity with the Orthodox church means to him, and how passionately he desires to overcome the Church's schism of 1054. In his address, the pope said, "We are entering a new phase of our reconciliation, with the joint determination to have it be the final phase."[41]

There is no doubt that at the present stage, the Roman Catholic church, especially through the initiative of Pope John Paul II, is concentrating its ecumenical efforts on the Orthodox churches with the greatest expectations. Pope John Paul II spoke of unification with the church of the East by the beginning of the third millennium. There is not much time left till then, and one should have no illusions about just how difficult the dialogues are going to be, especially on the subject of the jurisdictional primacy of the pope. This has already been demonstrated in the meetings of the International Orthodox–Catholic Commission, the last one in Munich in 1982: "We are still at the beginning." The Orthodox will not accept a primacy in the sense of an explicit adoption of the Vatican I formulation. Only one solution is conceivable, as Ratzinger proposed:

> Rome must not require more of a primacy doctrine from the East than was formulated and experienced in the first millennium. In Phanar, on 25 July 1976, when Patriarch Athenagoras addressed the visiting pope as Peter's successor, the first in honor among us, and the presider over charity, this great church leader was expressing the essential content of the declarations on the primacy of the first millennium. And Rome cannot ask for more. Unification could occur if the East abandons its attacks on the Western development of the second millennium as being heretical, and accepts the Catholic church as legitimate and orthodox in the form which it experienced in its own development. Conversely, unification could occur if the West recognized the Eastern church as orthodox and legitimate in the form in which it has maintained itself.[42]

(b) When stating the problem regarding the churches of the Reformation, several important documents must be mentioned: the issue of the papacy is touched on in the so-called *Malta Document* of 1972,[43] which the delegates of the Lutheran World Council and the Roman Secretariat on Unity published under the title *The Gospel and the Church*. The statement is made that the jurisdictional primacy must, above all, "be understood as service to the community and as bond of the unity of the Church" (168). The office of the pope also includes the task of caring for the legitimate diversity of the local churches.

The actual form of this office can vary greatly, depending on the respective historical circumstances. The Lutherans conceded that no local church can isolate itself, since it is the manifestation of the universal Church. This is the sense in which the importance of the church's service to the community is regarded; and, at the same time, the problem which the lack of effective service to unity creates for Lutherans is pointed out. Thus the office of the pope as visible sign of the unity of the churches was found acceptable, insofar as it is subjected to the primacy of the gospel by means of theological reinterpretation and factual restructuring.

However, the question of whether the primacy of the pope is necessary for the Church or whether it merely portrays a possible function in principle remains a matter of controversy between Catholics and Lutherans. But it can be said that, if the pope's primacy function can be acknowledged as a possibility, and if this possibility is truly realized (in the sense of this thesis), then (in the sense of Thesis II) no explicit confession of dogmatic necessity of the primacy of the pope should be required of the Protestant partner churches of the one Church.

The question of the papacy was dealt with more thoroughly and extensively in the Lutheran–Roman Catholic Dialogue group for the United States, an official group consisting of theologians and bishops, in the document *Papal Primacy and the Church Universal. Differing Attitudes Toward Papal Primacy* (1974).[44] The document carefully discusses the exegetical and historical problems connected with this issue, and justifiably points out that the facts unearthed are assessed differently by the Protestant-Lutheran and the Catholic perspectives as a result of their respective a priori presuppositions. The most important statements in the document refer to future prospects, under the heading "Toward the Renewal of Papal Structures."[45]

If the papacy, both at present and in future, is to gain ecumenical significance, and if it is to serve the Church as a whole better and more effectively, then, so it is said, a renewal of its structure, or rather structures, is necessary. These structures should be oriented to the principles of legitimate diversity, collegiality, and subsidiarity. It is clear that these are principles which understand the papacy to be in the "inside" of the Church, and wish to see it realized. One is—justifiably—convinced that a supreme office of unity can only fulfill its potential and carry out its tasks if it abandons a centralized and isolated form, stops wanting to accomplish everything single-

71

handedly, and if it affirms not only in theory but also in practice the reality which is suitable to the shape of the Church. This is the reality of a unity which finds in legitimate diversity not a hindrance but the living expression of unity. It is a reality which can acknowledge the significance of the "first" only if the reason why the pope should be the first is defined and recognized. This is collegiality on the various rungs and levels of the Church and in the Church, all of whom bear responsibility, in their own fashion, as the people of God. Furthermore, it is the legitimate diversity of the churches—the unity of which the pope should protect.

The principle of subsidiarity is the result of legitimate diversity and collegiality. It relieves the "head," and it reveals the liveliness as well as the richness of the variety. And this is precisely what can contribute to the liveliness and edification of the Church.

A renewal in the structures of the papacy should be carried out on the basis of these principles. The differentiation between supreme authority and its use enables the pope to limit the exercise of his jurisdiction voluntarily. This would produce a differentiation with regard to the functions of the papacy which would make a larger "ecumenicity" conceivable. For the same reason, and with reference to the same principles, the result would be that the pope's primacy would be more a preeminence of pastoral care than a juridical primacy with its typical problems of rights, of powers, and of qualifications. The necessity and (inner) limitation of the remaining juridical aspects would be rendered comprehensible precisely on the basis of the pope's pastoral duty.

According to the Lutheran members who contributed to this document, there is no reason to reject a supreme office of unity of the Church if these principles are recognized and realized. The good sense, the significance, and the "blessing" of such an office is increasingly recognized and clearly affirmed exactly in today's Christendom which is striving for unity. The only requirement deemed necessary by the Protestant participants is that "the papal primacy be constituted, understood, and above all perceived in such a way that this office unambiguously serve the gospel and the unity of Christians, and that the exercise of its power not subvert Christian freedom." It is clear that the intentions of the Reformation are being expressed.

The declaration of consensus was followed by the explicit statement that it is of secondary importance to the basic issue to speak of either divine or human right in relation to the papacy. Formulating, and thus restricting, the issue in terms of divine or human right would render ecumenical progress impossible and result in discussions which could never be settled. However, in accordance with our Thesis II, the question of "divine right (*ius divinum*)" or "human right (*ius humanum*)" does not even have to be decided.

The writers of the document then address the churches with a plea to undertake concrete steps toward reconciliation.

> Therefore we ask the Lutheran churches whether they are prepared to confirm that papal primacy, renewed in the light of the Gospel, need not be a hindrance to reconciliation. We ask further whether they are able not only to recognize the legitimacy of the papal office in the service of the Roman Catholic church, but also to recognize the feasibility and desirability of the papal office, renewed under the Gospel, in the service of a more inclusive community which would include the Lutheran churches.

But the Roman Catholic church is also asked whether, for the sake of reconciliation, it is willing to open discussions on possible structures which would protect the legitimate traditions of the Lutheran churches and respect their intellectual heritage. Furthermore, it is asked whether, in the expectation of a foreseeable reconciliation, it is prepared to acknowledge the Lutheran churches represented in our dialogue as sister churches which already possess the right to a certain amount of ecclesiastical community.

The document closes with:

> We believe that our joint statement reflects a convergence in the theological understanding of the papacy which makes possible a fruitful approach to these questions. Our churches should not miss this occasion to respond to the will of Christ for the unity of his disciples. Neither church should continue to tolerate a situation in which the members of one community look upon the other as alien. Trust in the Lord, who makes us one body in Christ, will help us to risk ourselves on yet undisclosed paths toward which His Holy Spirit is guiding His church.[46]

However, this remarkable document has not yet received an official ecclesiastical confirmation. That did not prevent this dialogue group from continuing, and turning its attention to the theme of papal infallibility, and declaring, "this apparently unresolved question need not be a hindrance to reconciliation between the Lutheran and the Catholic church."[47]

With regard to our topic, the *Protestant (Evangelischer) Adult Catechism,* published at the request of the United Evangelical-Lutheran church of Germany, states:

> According to the New Testament, all the apostles have a fundamental significance for the Church. Peter is their representative. Even though the foundation has been laid only once, one can ask whether the service of one representative and spokesman for all of Christianity is not meaningful later too . . . However, until now the non-Roman churches have not presented a convincing model for how the unity of the Church could attain a visible form . . . The attitude of the other churches toward the papacy will depend in large measure on whether Rome will succeed in presenting the papacy convincingly as such a *service to unity* and as sign of unity.[48]

Wolfhart Pannenberg expressed himself in similar fashion: he recommended that the pope's claim to serve the faith, to be the center of unity, and to be the shepherd and teacher of all believers be taken at face value. He calls attention to one consequence, which he formulates in this way:

> If the competent authority especially responsible for the unity of all of Christianity already exists in the person of the bishop of Rome, should not the unification of the separated churches be the primary and most urgent concern of the pope? Should he not consider the needs and problems, but also the possible positive contribution of the Christians still separated from Rome, in all his decisions and proclamations, instead of concerning himself solely with the preservation of the church now calling itself Catholic, and of its members in the faith of the Apostles? Much, perhaps of decisive importance for the cause of Christian unity, would be won if, on every occasion and in full public view, the pope made it clear that he is taking up the cause of all Christians—even those Christians still separated from Rome at present—and if by his conduct he demonstrated the fellowship in Christ which binds all Christians to each other. To the same degree that the Roman bishop allows the present problems and ways of thinking, as well as the possible contributions of the other churches to the life of today's Christianity, to penetrate his thinking and his decisions, and expresses them, to that degree could his claim to be the representative

of all of Christianity gain credibility even outside today's Roman Catholic church. The example of John XXIII demonstrates the actual possibilities open to us along this line.[49]

There is no doubt that *The Final Report* of the official Commission for the Anglican–Roman Catholic Dialogue, the *Windsor Declaration* (1981)—the result of nine years of continuous work—represents the greatest convergence and agreement to date on the subject of the papacy. The commission speaks of a "substantial agreement." The point of departure and the perspective of the *Declaration* is the conception of Church as "*koinonia,*" as "*communio,*" which is also the basic definition of the Vatican II ecclesiology. In this connection, the *Declaration* states:

All servants of the gospel must be in community with each other, for the one Church is a community of local churches. Just so must they be united in the Apostolic faith. As a focal point within the *koinonia*, a primacy is the guarantee that what they teach and do is in harmony with the faith of the Apostles . . . [50]

Unity is the essence of the Church. Since the Church is visible, unity must be visible. Full, visible community between our churches cannot be achieved without mutual recognition of the sacraments and of the ministerial office, together with the joint acceptance of a universal primacy which, in connection with the College of Bishops, is a servant to unity. (No. 9)[51]

We agree that a universal primacy will be required in a reunited church, and that this should appropriately be the primacy of the Bishop of Rome. In a reunited church, an office formed on the basis of Peter's role will be sign and guarantor of such unity.[52]

The text states, with reference to the Vatican I thesis—which became the thesis of Catholic theology—that the primacy of the pope is based on divine right because it was instituted by Jesus Christ:

It is the sign of visible *koinonia* which God desires for His church, and through which unity in diversity is realized. The qualification "iure divino" can be applied to a universal primacy regarded in this way within the collegiality of bishops and the *koinonia* of the whole church. (No. 11)[53]

In the past, Anglicans have considered the Roman Catholic doctrine, that the Bishop of Rome is the universal Primate on the basis of divine laws, to be unacceptable. Yet we believe that the primacy of the Bishop of Rome can be understood as part of God's plan for universal *koino-*

nia, in a manner which can be reconciled with both our traditions. In view of this consensus, the figure of speech "divine law" which Vatican I uses, need not be considered a reason for differences of opinion between us. (No. 15)[54]

This sentence is explained in the following manner: "According to Christian doctrine, the unity of Christian community requires visible expression. We agree that such a visible expression is the will of God, and that the preservation of visible unity on the universal level encompasses the episcopate of a universal primacy. That is a doctrinal statement."[55]

The jurisdiction to which the statement on primacy refers is "described as the power required to exercise an office." Certain orientations are connected to this which could be given in the performance of the primacy. That is why the text demands:

> The universal Primate should exercise his office recognizably to all, not in isolation but in collegial association with the bishops. This in no way lessens his own responsibility to speak and to act on behalf of the whole church on occasion. The responsibility to provide for the universal Primate's universal jurisdiction is supported with every bishop's office. Yet the universal Primate in not the source from which the diocesan bishops derive their authority. Nor does his authority undermine that of the Metropolitan or diocesan bishop. The primacy is not an autocratic authority over the church; rather, it is a service within the church to the church which understands itself to be a community of local churches in faith and in love. (No. 19)[56]

Derived from this are certain moral limits to the exercise of the universal primacy:

> The jurisdiction of the universal primacy has its meaning in the primacy's capability to promote catholicity as well as unity, and to cultivate and assemble the treasures of the various traditions of the churches. The collegial and primatial responsibility for the preservation of the particular life of local churches requires the appropriate respect for their customs and traditions in so far as they do not contradict the faith or destroy the community. Striving for unity must not be separated from providing for catholicity. (No. 21)[57]

The demand that freedom of conscience not be endangered is also made.

If, as happens here, primacy is derived from the essence of the church, and if this essence is regarded as having been established in the Will of God through the cross and resurrection, then one can discern in the primacy an origin established in Jesus Christ. One can call this origin "divine law (*ius divinum*)" even when this divine law is not based on one of Jesus' explicit, juridically formulated words of institution.

No more can and no more need be said on the subject of the origin of papal primacy in the dialogue between the churches—either by looking at the biblical and historical situation or by looking at the status of contemporary ecumenical theology. The Anglicans say no less about the meaning, right, and reason of the primacy than the churches of the East—rather more, in fact.

According to Ratzinger, one may in no way consider the nineteenth and twentieth century form of primacy (both explicit doctrine and the application of it *iure humano*) to be the only possible and required form for all Christians. Therefore it is inadmissable to compare the statements in the Anglican–Roman Catholic *Final Report* only to the statements of Vatican I, to judge them by Vatican I, and to check whether they agreed with the terminology and requirements of Vatican I—which is what the Roman *Congregation of the Faith* did in its response. To do that is to transform Vatican I into an absolute and unhistorical entity.

Ratzinger states that the maximal demand the West could make of the East would be to require their recognition of the primacy of the Roman bishop in the entirety of its definition of 1870. This would require the East to make room for a practice of primacy like the one accepted by the Uniate churches. Regarding this and other maximal demands, he declares, "none of the maximal solutions contains a real hope for unity." Should not what is true for Orthodoxy also hold true for Anglicans?

The text of the Anglican–Roman Catholic *Final Report* also deals with the issue of the infallibility of the papal office in an extremely remarkable fashion. Here too the *Report*'s point of departure is the Church as a whole, the Church as *koinonia*. The Church as a whole is witness, teacher, and guardian of truth. It lives in the confidence that the Holy Spirit effectively places it in a position to fulfill its mission, so that it can neither lose its essential character nor miss its goal.

The preservation of the Church in truth makes it necessary for the Church at certain moments to make decisive judgments regarding essential questions of the dogma which will become a part of its enduring testimony. The Thirty-nine Articles make clear that this is in accordance with Anglican faith: "The Church has authority in controversial issues regarding faith." Such a judgment clarifies what the truth is, and strengthens the Church's certitude in the proclamation of the gospel (no. 24).[58]

> The Church exercises its teaching authority through diverse instruments and authorities at various levels. When matters of faith are at stake, the Church can arrive at decisions regarding them at General Councils; we are in agreement that these decisions are binding. We have also acknowledged that a united Church needs a universal Primate who presides over the *koinonia* and can therefore speak with binding authority in the name of the Church. The Church can arrive at a decisive verdict in matters of faith through these two authorities, and can thus exclude error. (No. 26)[59]

This service is not meant to supplement the content of revelation. It should instead recall and emphasize an important truth: "to expose error, bring to light insufficiently recognized consequences, and make clear how Christian truth should be applied to contemporary matters" (no. 27).[60] One must, however, remember that these definitions were produced by specific historical situations, and that they are always shaped by the understanding and conditions of their time. "Yet if they protect the substance of faith, they have an enduring significance in the lasting life of the Church."[61]

The defining teaching judgment of the pope is tied to a whole set of strict conditions: "he must speak explicitly as focal point within the *koinonia*; he must not be subject to coercion by outside pressure; he must have been careful to gather the opinion of his fellow bishops and of the church as a whole; and he must clearly announce his intention to present a binding decision in matters of faith and morals." The "irreformable" part of his judgment means "that the truth which has been expressed in the definition can no longer be called into question." It does not mean that the definition is the church's final word or that the definition cannot be put in different words (no. 29).[62]

The Roman Catholic tradition has used the term 'infallibility" to describe the guaranteed freedom from basic error in teaching judgments. In the Roman Catholic dogma, infallibility means merely the protection of the teaching judgment against error for the sake of sustaining the church in truth. It does not mean a positive inspiration or revelation. In addition, the infallibility ascribed to the bishop of Rome represents a gift which enables him—in certain circumstances and under precisely delineated conditions—to be an instrument of the infallibility of the Church. We are in agreement that this term can be applied, in its unrestricted sense, only to God, and that its application to a human being—even under extremely limited conditions—can give rise to many misunderstandings. For this reason we have avoided using that term when we express our faith in the preservation of the Church against error. The fact that under certain conditions infallibility was ascribed to the bishop of Rome contributed—we jointly acknowledge this also—in large measure to giving all his pronouncements an exaggerated significance. (No. 32)[63]

Nevertheless, the *Report* concludes with a common statement that the church needs a pluriform and extensive authority in which all members of God's people participate, as well as a universal primacy which is servant and focal point of the visible unity of truth and love. This does not mean that all differences were resolved; "yet if a Petrine function or a Petrine office in the living church is exercised at all, in which a universal Primate is called to serve as visible focal point, then it is a part of his office to have a clearly delineated responsibility for dogma as well as the appropriate gifts of the Spirit which enable him to realize it."[64]

The response of the Roman *Congregation of the Faith* states that the concept "indefectibility" is not synonymous with the concept "infallibility" set by Vatican I. But should one not rather ask whether the matter under discussion must be connected to the concept "infallibility" at all—to a concept which, according to today's understanding, calls forth the most extreme implications which are completely beside the point? What is meant is preservation from error. The word "infallible" is a misleading word. One should not cling to it with every means. Rather, one should replace it with a less misleading concept, one more conducive to consensus; at least, one should clarify it, perhaps with the concept "truth" or "the ultimate commitment" of such a definition. Despite their agreement regarding the necessity for a universal primacy in a reunited Church, the Anglicans cannot agree with the notion that an almost a priori part of the office of the bishop of Rome is the guaranteed possession of a gift of divine assistance in making judgments on dogma, "by virtue of which his formal decisions can count as fully safeguarded preceding their reception by the believers."

Increased attention is being given to the *problem of reception* in today's theology. G. Kretschmar speaks of a circle: "The whole church accepts something which the Council formulated as truth; that it can do so is possible only under the presupposition of its orthodoxy. The circle can be dissolved only because the same Spirit of God is at work in both (Council and whole church) and because both Council and the receiving church know they are subject to the Apostolic word."[65]

The same principle can be applied with regard to the definition of the pope "ex cathedra." What is at stake in the process of reception is not a mechanical acceptance or reception, but communication—the living actualization and adoption of what is presented as binding on faith. Reception will not be made an internal constitutive element of the legitimate papal teaching judgment; but Catholics can say that reception can be viewed as the surest sign that in actuality it is a matter of a true and binding teaching judgment subject to the special promise of Christ. Catholics can add that this judgment has thus fulfilled the necessary conditions to be a true expression of faith. After all, *Lumen Gentium* (no. 25) says that the assent (*assensus*) of the church must accompany papal definitions.[66] But since it is not always easy to determine which authority (there being levels) a pope actually used in his teaching, this problem can certainly also be solved on the basis of the existence or nonexistence of a general assent of the church.

It is certainly correct to agree with Ratzinger that the pope does not "merely ratify processes of reception, but instead has the right, against the background of the church's faith, to definitive decisions and definitive interpretations."[67]

Precisely this background is the issue. And why this obvious reversion of the pope's decision to the faith of the church (he certainly receives no new revelation) should not be made as clear and as transparent to the church as possible is totally incomprehensible. But perhaps the reception referred to here means not much more than the background indispensable to a definitive doctrinal decision. In other words, it means the context of faith which takes verbal form in a possible papal definition, for this should be expression and voice only of the faith the church believes.

In my controversy with Hans Küng I contested his thesis asserting the existence of a priori papal doctrinal decisions guaranteed from the start to be infallible. The pope's decisions ensue a posteriori from the revelation preceding them and from the church's faith in them which has been given to the church. Vatican II explains, "In this case the bishop of Rome does not present his decision as a private person. Instead, he interprets Catholic dogma and protects it, in his capacity as supreme teacher of the whole church. He alone has received the charisma of the infallibility of the church itself" (*Lumen Gentium*, no. 25).[68]

That is not contradicted by the fact that Vatican I had explained that the official doctrinal decisions of the pope are irrevocable out of himself, not in consequence of the agreement of the church (*ex sese, non ex consensu ecclesiae irreformabiles*). This sentence has an anti-Gallican point, and repudiates the opinion that an ex cathedra papal definition, made under the necessary specified conditions, should subsequently once again be submitted to another *juridical* authority such as a national Bishops' Conference. However, who detects the historical background of this formulation—incorporated without comment in Vatican II—without understanding "not from the consent of the church (*non ex consensu ecclesiae*)" to mean that the pope is isolated from and independent of the church when making his decisions?[69]

These detailed explanations should illustrate and give the reasons why this thesis can be erected today: all partner churches acknowledge the meaning and right of the Petrine service of the Roman pope to be the concrete guarantor of the unity of the Church in truth and love. The partner churches were represented and had a chance to be heard, though in somewhat fragmentary fashion. The presuppositions and conditions for this thesis are contained in all of this.

The demands that the partner churches make on the structure and function of the primacy in the form of jurisdiction and teaching office—collegiality, subsidiarity, obedience to the gospel, and respect for the freedom of conscience—not only accord with the demand for a church constantly to be reformed (*ecclesia semper reformanda*) in the actuality of the papacy, which is to be understood as Petrine service. They are also in accordance with the principles and demands of the Catholic church itself, which expressed them in Vatican II especially. The same applies to the infallibility established by the whole Church, as it is actualized in the teaching office of the pope. One can only hope that the communities already produced among the churches will attain an ever more convincing actualization in practice.

At the conclusion of this chapter, I would like to pose the following summary question to the non–Roman Catholic churches: Do these churches consider the Roman Catholic doctrine regarding the function of the pope—as we understand it today and as Rome already practices it (even though it is in need of correction)—a doctrine and practice so radically contradictory to the essence of the Protestant message that they must reject this doctrine and practice as a deadly contradiction to their faith and as an extreme threat to their eternal salvation? If they do not dare say that, the plain question is why they do not want to live together with us Catholics in the one Church, since this Church (as will be shown even more clearly, and as has been shown in Thesis II and III) in practice demands no more than what is already being lived out in the relationship of its members to its officials.

THESIS IVb

The pope, for his part, explicitly commits himself to acknowledge and to respect the thus agreed-upon independence of the partner churches. He declares (by human right, iure humano) that he will make use of his highest teaching authority (ex cathedra), granted to him in conformity with Catholic principles by the First Vatican Council, only in a manner that conforms juridically or in substance to a general council of the whole Church, just as his previous ex cathedra decisions have been issued in agreement and close contact with the whole Catholic episcopate.

Thesis IVa stated that the other large Christian churches and communities which wish to unite with the Roman Catholic church must recognize the Petrine office as an entity also binding on themselves, in order to achieve a true unity of the churches, which results in more than a World Council of Churches. Conversely, Thesis IVb describes how the pope, for his part, must contribute to this recognition of his significance and function in the one Church.

I

One should not consider the requirements of Theses IVa and IVb a "*do ut des*," a trade and a compromise, which would ultimately be a matter of options. Even under the condition of what was said in Thesis II and Thesis IVa about the particular way the Roman primacy and its teaching office should be acknowledged, such an acknowledgment of the Petrine office in the one Church on the part of non–Roman Catholic churches signifies a decision of faith. It means the assent to the reality of this office in the one Church which is affirmed as the actuality of faith, even though what must be so explicitly acknowledged is not identical, as was said before, with positive and explicit recognition of the teaching of Vatican I.

On the other hand, papal acknowledgment of the permanent independence of the partner churches in the one Church, as stated in this thesis, is certainly an acknowledgment which, from the essence of the church, the pope is clearly committed to make. This acknowledgment, as formal principle of ecclesiology, certainly is not subject to the pope's wishes.

That does not mean that a more precise adjustment of the relationship between unity of the Church and the pope's universal ecclesial function on the one hand, and the independence of the partner churches in actual delimitations on the other, cannot be determined in a variety of ways. It is, in fact, variable (as church history has shown), and to a certain extent can also be determined by the pope according to his own decision, as Rome is demonstrating by its actual behavior toward the Uniate Eastern churches. To this extent, the more exact delimitation between the unity of the Church and Roman primacy on the one hand, and the independence of the partner churches on the other, is a matter of actual arrangements of a historically variable kind, regarding which Rome and the partner churches uniting with Rome must freely reach an agreement.

A fundamental and formal justification for, and recognition of, the independence of the partner churches by Rome is not simply subject to Rome's wishes, but is instead (if one wants to express it this way) "of divine right (*iuris divini*)." Therefore, the partner churches desiring to unite with Rome definitely have a right to judge whether the actual (variable, and basically changeable in future) delimitation established between the two entities—both of which must be respected—really signifies a sufficient realization of the fundamental right of independence. To that extent, therefore, it is perfectly legitimate, in negotiations for unity, to have Rome explain how it actually envisions acknowledging the independence of the partner churches in the future of the one Church. By doing that, Rome fulfills a condition under which the other side can in faith acknowledge the right of the primacy.

The kind of particularity corresponding to the diversity of the partner churches which want to unite with Rome, and corresponding to their respective history and actual constitutions, has a different relationship to the particularity of the existing Roman Catholic church which, with its own particularity, would become one of the many partner churches at the time of unification. That is why the "concession" to the various particularities that Rome makes and declares, in order to become the head of all partner churches (just as the Latin Western church already constitutes only a part of the whole Roman Catholic church, since the Uniate Eastern churches are also a part of the Roman Catholic church) will be formulated differently. Thus they will be the subject of a variety of agreements

Rome makes with these different partner churches. In any case, such "concessions" are perfectly in accord with the doctrine of Vatican I regarding the primacy of the pope, and they do not lessen Rome's rank.

In the many concordats with secular states that Rome has concluded for many centuries up to the present day, Rome has always declared itself ready to respect certain rights and liberties of nations, which are not compellingly necessary to recognize in detail, but which Rome nevertheless in fact recognizes. Thus these practical types of delimitations agreed on by treaty are surely possible between Rome and individual partner churches also. In concordats between the Holy See and secular nations, it is frequently a question of actual rights and liberties conceded to the partner churches of the nation concerned. But that means that Rome can make such "concessions" to that partner church directly.

We cannot describe here just what such agreements regarding these delimitations would look like in detail. Precise delimitations could only be arrived at between Rome and the respective partner churches if previous negotiations had thoroughly examined the respective "canon law" of a partner church. This examination would determine whether that "canon law" could remain in force, or whether and to what extent it should be modified to make this existing law, as the law of one partner church in the one Church, congruent with its Petrine office.

In any case, the following theses contain a few more indications of a general nature on how the individual autonomy of the partner churches could be reconciled with the primacy of the pope, and therefore could and should be specifically acknowledged by Rome.

II

In this connection, a particular arrangement should be made with regard to the specific manner of exercising the Roman *teaching primacy*. If there is a Petrine office which has a particular task and function for the unity of the Church in truth, then Rome can and should (leaving aside particular ex cathedra decisions for the moment) certainly assume such a task vis-à-vis all these partner churches in the future as well. This does not simply and clearly mean that this task must be carried out in exactly the fashion that

Rome has thus far performed it in the Roman Catholic church. Why should there not be papal "encyclicals" in future, addressed to all these partner churches? One must, however, expect that these encyclicals, in their composition, must take into account the great dissimilarity in the mentality and in the religious and theological thinking of these very different addressees, and must therefore find appropriate formulations.

Nor can one conceive of Rome being able to dispense with some kind of institutionalization in the performance of its task of tending the unity and purity of faith in the whole Church and therefore in all partner churches. There will have to be some kind of institution in Rome analogous to today's *Congregation of the Faith* in the one Church of the future. However, this future *Congregation of the Faith* would have to be structured and filled in such a way as to be able to perform its task while recognizing the theological peculiarities of the individual partner churches.

In the existing Roman Catholic church, one can already have justified expectations which have not been met with respect to the structure, composition, procedure, and transparency of the proceedings of the *Congregation of the Faith*. Therefore a future *Congregation of the Faith* in the one and very varied Church will have to be quite different from the present *Congregation of the Faith*. It is quite conceivable that true respect for the particularity of the partner churches means that the future *Congregation of the Faith* will at all times exert its influence on the individual partner churches, and on their individual teachers and doctrines, only by way of the bishops of these partner churches.

The actual practice of the Roman primacy of teaching naturally needs a particular arrangement in those cases which pertain to ex cathedra decisions of the Roman pope in the meaning of both Vatican I and Vatican II. For one thing, the pope's fundamental right to make ex cathedra decisions may not be contested in the one Church to be either, in so far as they apply to all the partner churches in principle, even though the actual agreement of this principle with Thesis II needs further examination. It is also conceivable, in the abstract and in principle, that the pope would decide matters of faith (for example, particular linguistic regulations) for the Western partner church—he is its patriarch, after all—in differentiation from his uni-

86

versal function for the whole Church, and that these decisions directly affect only the Western partner church over which he presides as patriarch. (It is also conceivable that an episcopal, or even patriarchic leader of another partner church makes such teaching decisions, which apply directly only to his own church, since such a leader of a partner church also possesses and must exercise a teaching authority granted to him by virtue of his own office and not really by delegation from the pope.)

Now, it has always been obvious in the existing Roman Catholic church that the actual practice of a defining teaching primacy of the pope is tied to essential provisions, because the pope does not receive new revelations. Instead he is bound to traditional revelation and can make decisions only within the religious consciousness of the whole church. Nor is its obviousness lessened by the fact that the fulfilling of these necessary conditions for the pope's ex cathedra decisions cannot be tested by another juridical "higher" authority, and therefore the binding quality of the pope's decision does not depend on the successful results of such a juridical test. But, on the other hand, it must be admitted that these conditions (the application of every required and feasible human means beforehand in order to justify such an ex cathedra decision) are not expressed very clearly or distinctly in the official ecclesiastical exposition of the teaching primacy and its practice. However, it is possible to do so, and that could overcome the distrust of the still-separated churches, which fear that by acknowledging the Roman teaching primacy they would be signing a blank check. Furthermore, it would be impossible to predict how Rome might write out such a blank check in future ex cathedra decisions. But this could give rise to situations in which their own religious consciousness would force these churches to refuse to consent to such a teaching decision, which would be contrary to the given fundamental recognition of the Roman teaching primacy. This fear could certainly be overcome more easily if the actual manner of arriving at such a teaching decision were explained with absolute clarity and were made transparent.

Both papal ex cathedra decisions in the nineteenth and twentieth centuries were arrived at by surveying all the bishops of the Roman Catholic church in a way that should completely sweep away the fear that Rome's arbitrary decisions would violate the religious consciousness in partner churches. Moreover, one should count on the fact that, of all the future bishops of the whole Church—all of whom would be surveyed—a large number would be bishops representing those partner churches that had had a different theological way of thinking and a different tradition before they united with Rome into one Church.

What was in fact practiced in the nineteenth and twentieth centuries with regard to ex cathedra decisions can also be codified juridically. Rome could explicitly formulate this codification, and recognize it as legitimate law, even if the actual procedural details of arriving at a papal ex cathedra decision were obviously by human law (*ius humanum*) in the church. These details could also be modified in future to accord with the intellectual-political and theological circumstances of that time. Juridical provisions should be made to assure the transparency of any future survey of all the bishops in the future Church, which was not yet done in a desirable way in the surveys conducted with regard to the definition of the immaculate conception and of the bodily assumption of Mary into heaven.

Such a transparent survey need not necessarily mean that future definitions would be juridically possible only by a vote of all the bishops, as though in a true council. Even under the condition of a survey, the pope could still issue definitions by virtue of the power granted him as pope, in distinction from the rest of the bishops. Moreover, it is obvious that an official and therefore binding declaration by all the bishops on the basis of their teaching authority is possible only if the pope concurs in such a declaration. And he cannot be overruled. Thus the distinction between papal teaching authority in a council and papal teaching authority "alone" is a conceptually subtle matter, the significance of which cannot be overestimated.

III

With regard to the issue of the future significance of the defining teaching primacy of the pope, the following must also be considered so as to avoid the impression that still-separated churches, when acknowledging this teaching primacy, would plunge into the adventure of a future history of religion which they would not dare to embark upon. It is inconceivable that a future history of the practice of the Roman defining teaching primacy would consist of an endless series of ever-new definitions on the basis of papal teaching authority. The permanence of a teaching authority in the future Church in no way means that the actual circumstances in which it can be exercised will always remain the same, thus making definitions actually possible.

The future history of revelation and the history of religion need not necessarily consist of ever-new differentiations of the original substance of faith, as the conventional Catholic theory of the history of doctrine has thought since the nineteenth century. Not only is this theory problematic in itself, it is also definitely conceivable that in future there will be fewer situations, if any, in which logical differentiations of earlier dogma could be put into definitions. And if one presupposes other theories of the history of dogma, as they have been developed quite recently, then it is even less conceivable that actual possibilities for new definitions can be derived from them in future. They could not even approximately be understood as supplementary declarations to the existing content of faith.

Human beings live in the pluralistic intellectual situation which we referred to in the Commentary to Thesis II. A global Church contains an unavoidable plurality of theologies which must be "accultured" differently everywhere. Today and in future the Church is expected to carry on the pressing argument with a worldwide and militant atheism. For all these reasons, it is extremely unlikely that the Roman teaching office will in future still issue definitions (like the definition of the immaculate conception and the bodily assumption of Mary into heaven) which—at least at first glance—seem to be definite additions to the existing substance of faith (although on closer examination this proves to have been not the case at all).

The pope's function in matters of faith—with regard to possible definitions—will in future be the preservation and the clarification, appropriate to the situation, of *the* substance of faith already expressed in the ancient creeds (see Thesis I). He will do this not because the formal range (if one may say it this way) of the papal teaching authority in matters of faith was limited from the very beginning, but because the intellectual situation—which is the precondition for the exercise of papal teaching authority—requires this kind of preserving, protecting, and reformulating function of the teaching authority both today and in future. But this same situation also makes an apparently additive and differentiating exercise of this teaching authority impossible in practice.

If one expected, or thought it desirable, that the pope issue real ex cathedra decisions as often as possible—which the opponents to papal teaching authority had feared and predicted at the time of Vatican I—one would not only contradict the experience of history since Vatican I, one would diminish instead of increasing the importance of the papal teaching office. However, one could understand the pope's authority (an authority which should be neither denied nor obscured) for the future to make ex cathedra decisions in this functional and rational way. Then one could also say that, without diminishing or endangering his teaching authority, the pope can, by human law (*iure humano*), make explicit, and acknowledge, the procedures of this teaching authority, which can remove the fear of non–Roman Catholic Christians that acknowledging papal teaching authority would put them in danger of being confronted later with new papal definitions. Their Christian religious conscience would not permit them to accept these definitions (in contradistinction to other authentic but nondefining doctrinal declarations of the pope) because they would then be required to give an absolute affirmation of faith, which they could not give. In practice, a defining declaration of faith from the Roman teaching office—in case it would be issued in the future—would expect nothing from them which has not always really been their own Christian conviction.

Performing the papal teaching authority in authentic and nondefining declarations does not threaten (if one may put it this way) the religious conscience of Christians of Reformation background in the one Church. It has always been clear in Catholic traditional teaching that it is entirely possible to refuse to affirm such declarations if, after testing them thoroughly, one finds them erroneous, because they are not required to be free of error from the very beginning or forever. That was also explicitly stated in a joint pastoral letter by the German bishops in 1967.

To say this in no way means that the merely authentic and nondefining doctrinal declarations of the Holy See are of no importance to Protestant Christians or theologians. These declarations normally have significant content and essential weight, which speaks for them. They also have a formal authority, even if they are not "infallible"—an authority which can and must be respected, even if it is not absolute. A Protestant theologian does not treat the Augsburg Confession in the same way he treats a book by any one of his colleagues either.

However, one will have to add that the description—in *Lumen Gentium*, no. 25, and in can. 752 of the new *Canon Law*—of the attitude of a theologian vis-à-vis authentic but nondefining doctrinal declarations of Rome is an inadequate and insufficiently differentiated description. Moreover, any progress, or overturning of erroneous declarations (which can be done also) of the Roman teaching office would be impossible if, always and in every case, a theologian's only permitted response to such declarations were "a religious perception and pious submission of mind and will (*religiosum intellectus et voluntatis obsequium*)," and never a critical stance which excludes this affirmation.

One could ask more precisely if it is impossible to conceive of a case where not just one individual Christian in one of the partner churches announces his reservations about an authentic but nondefining declaration of the pope (which is also conceivable within the Roman partner church), but where a whole partner church declares it cannot agree with that teaching declaration. Such a case is not entirely impossible in a global Church with great cultural differences among the regional partner churches, especially with regard to ethical questions. One can more easily imagine disagreements on ethical questions because of the different cultural environments of the partner churches. Yet one should not overestimate this danger either.

The various partner churches will participate in Rome's teaching declarations from the very beginning if a correct structure of the future Roman *Congregation of the Faith* exists. Moreover, the theologians of the various partner churches will already have worked together to resolve the remaining problems since, despite their diversity and relative independence, these partner churches do not betoken ghettos to the individual theologians. Even in issues that do not involve definitions, contact between the pope and individual partner churches and their representatives will appropriately precede doctrinal declarations. It is therefore rather unlikely that very great difficulties will arise on this whole issue.

IV

Perhaps something can be added, in connection with the Commentary to Thesis IVb, about the most appropriate *papal election* in this Church composed of many partner churches, toward all of whom the pope is to exercise his Petrine service. According to Catholic ecclesiology, the pope is certainly identical (at least in fact) with the Roman bishop. But the Latin church as it is now constituted already has developed an election procedure to call the pope as supreme representative of the church. This procedure seeks to introduce him not only as bishop of Rome but as supreme leader of the whole church. The present College of Cardinals elects a man from among themselves who is chosen from the very beginning to be the leader of the whole church from the standpoint of the well being of the whole church, not merely the Roman bishopric.

It is obvious that, in the future Church composed of many partner churches, the method of election should be similar. The pope should be called *as* supreme head *of all* the partner churches; the method of electing him must be such that all partner churches can easily and eagerly acknowledge him as their head, even if, unavoidably, he can come from only one of these partner churches. Because it is a matter of human law (*ius humanum*), there are many conceivable methods of election, including appointment to the College of Election itself. Representatives of the various large partner churches could be represented in a College of Cardinals—if it is to continue to elect the pope—just as representatives of the large Bishops' Conferences attend the present College of Cardinals. But since today's papal Election Board is an arrangement of human law, a completely different election board could be thought of, such as one which from the very beginning is composed of representatives of the large partner churches, so that its members do not have to be appointed specifically by the pope. The pope at that time would still have appropriate influence on the calling of his successor, since these representatives of the large partner churches themselves would not hold their position without his agreement. (See Thesis V).

Other details of Thesis IVb probably do not require further explanations.

THESIS V

All partner churches, in accordance with ancient tradition, have bishops at the head of their larger subdivisions. The election of a bishop in these partner churches need not be done according to the normally valid manner in the Roman Catholic church. (The new Roman Canon Law also mentions ways of appointing a bishop other than through the pope's free choice. See can. 377, par. 1.)

I

It is fitting and meaningful to speak about bishops after statements on pope, Petrine office, and Petrine service in the Church of Christ. It is in bishops that the fact and the truth is made manifest that the Church exists in, and consists of, local churches (*Lumen Gentium*, no. 25). This applies not only to the Catholic church, but to all the churches which have charge of not only one local church but also have regional administration offices transcending the local, whatever that region may be called: bishopric, diocese, synod, territorial church, metropolis, patriarchate.

Just as the Petrine office is assigned to the whole church, and officiates therein, so is the office of the bishop assigned to the local churches, which are themselves subdivisions of partner churches. The bishop is the official head of a region encompassing and simultaneously integrating the local churches.

All churches, with the exception of some Congregationalist Free churches, have an episcopal structure and constitution: the Orthodox churches in an extremely pronounced fashion, but also the Roman Catholic church, the church of the Utrecht Union, the Old Catholic church, and the Anglican church. The issue of the validity of Anglican orders can be bracketed in this connection (see Thesis VII). Even the churches of the Reformation want to cling to the structure of bishops.[70]

The Lutheran churches of the Reformation started with the unity of the ecclesiastical office (of the ministry of the word [*ministerium verbi*]) and emphasized particularly the original unity of the office of bishops and presbyter contained in the New Testament and still witnessed in the early church. Yet the Reformers did not reject a division of the one ecclesiastical office into various services—as it has developed in the history of the church—especially the division into the offices of bishop, of presbyter, and of deacon. According to the Council of Trent, this division rests on divine command (DS 1776), whereas Vatican II—a noticeable difference—does attribute the one office of service to divine institution but, when referring to the three gradations, merely states that they have been so named since ancient times (*ab antiquo*) (*Lumen Gentium*, no. 28).[71] The Lutherans also expressed their willingness to allow the distinction between bishops and pastors through the right to ordain reserved to bishops.

But since the Catholic bishops at that time refused to ordain the Reformation preachers, the Reformers were confronted with an emergency: as a rule they ordained through ordained pastors, and thus laid claim to the episcopal structure of the office of pastors (ministers).

They believed that, on the authority of Jerome, they were justified to do this in such an emergency without violating the principle of apostolic succession of the ministerial office, by reason of the original unity of the office of bishop and presbyter. That is why Protestant theologians like Pannenberg make it a point to emphasize that what exists in the churches of the Reformation is not merely a succession in the faith of the apostles, "even though succession of the ministerial office has been interrupted." For, so it is said, if the chain of conferring offices is broken off, who ensures that we have the same understanding of faith, and that the course of our lives is in uninterrupted unity with the apostolic origin? That was in no way a matter of indifference to the Reformers. It is therefore important to note that they only took the step of ordaining pastors through pastors under the assumption that the authority of the ecclesiastical office, as of a bishop's office, is present in the pastors, and that the rest is a matter of church order which can one ignore in times of need. *emergency*

None of this excludes the fact that the Reformers speak of episcopal office by divine law. Although it is identical with the pastoral office, as service in the church, it simultaneously—albeit by human law—performs a function on the regional level in the form of overseeing, episcopacy, and visitation. Article 28 of the Augsburg Confession describes it this way:

It is the office of the bishop to preach the gospel, forgive sins, judge doctrine, and condemn doctrine that is contrary to the gospel, and exclude from the Christian community the ungodly whose wicked conduct is manifest. All this is to be done not by human power but by God's Word alone. On this account parishioners and churches are bound to be obedient to the bishops according to the saying of Christ, "He who hears you hears me" (Luke 10:16).[72]

The function of the church-governing office of the bishop survives in Protestant superintendents in a special way, so that A. von Campenhausen says, "With the word 'superintendent' (also *'superattendens'*) the Reformers not only adopted a Latin translation of the Greek *'episcopus'* they also clung to the bishop's office itself."[73] This is especially pronounced up to the present day in the Swedish Lutheran church. However, in the later consistorial orders of the territorial churches, the territorial sovereign was claimed as the emergency bishop; he was looked upon as successor to the Catholic bishop (*summepiscopat*) since the beginning of the seventeenth century. Only after 1918 was the way cleared for an ecclesiastical formation of the bishop's office in Germany.

Calvin tried to use the New Testament as a guide for his order of offices in a particular way: he related the office of pastors and doctors in Eph. 4:11 to the early church's office of presbyter, and, like the Augsburg Confession, he also cited Jerome as his authority and referred to the original unity of the office of bishop and presbyter. Calvin did not actually contest (*Präses*) the arrangement of higher offices either, although he tended to favor the arrangement of synods, because of the possible temptation of claims to power.

The Council of Trent expressed its views about the office of bishop. It speaks of the superiority of bishops over presbyters (DS 1777). This superiority consists in the circumstance that bishops have the power to confirm and ordain; the council explicitly denies that this authority is held jointly with presbyters. However, the council did not answer the controversial question of the time as to whether or not this superiority is by divine right.

In the doctrinal decree regarding the sacrament of ordination (DS 1768), the council adds that the superiority of bishops consists in the fact that they "possess a variety of other powers which others of inferior level of ordination [*inferioris ordinis*] have no right to exercise." According to this decree, the superiority also, and in particular, exists in the area of jurisdiction.

The Council of Trent did not take a clear position on the subject of the validity of the ministerial office in the Protestant-Lutheran congregations. "The rejection of the validity of the Lutheran offices is a widespread, virtually prevailing post-Tridentine doctrinal opinion, which relies on the Council of Trent but in no way must follow from it. The issue is not a binding Catholic doctrine, but rather a prevailing practice."[74] The issue of validity should be separated from the issue of orthodoxy, and is in no way resolved. That is demonstrated by the validity of baptism accepted by all churches when it is rightfully administered—in no matter which church.

Vatican II described the office and position of the bishop in detail (*Lumen Gentium*, chap. 3: *Christus Dominus*).[75]

Bishops are neither the pope's representatives nor his functionaries; they have their own, legitimate, regulated authority directly derived from Jesus Christ (*Lumen Gentium*, no. 28),[76] which the pope cannot abrogate and which he must respect. The pope is not an absolute monarch.[77]

Above all, bishops are seen as a college which has taken the place of the Apostles as shepherds of the Church. The position of the bishops is described through Luke 10:16 (*Lumen Gentium*, no. 29).[78] They possess the fullness of the sacrament of ordination; they are supervisors of the local churches in the tasks of sanctification, of teaching, and of leadership; their most important task is the proclamation of the gospel (no. 25).[79] Bishops represent the visible principle and foundation of unity in the partner churches, in and of which the Church exists. They are obligated to care for the whole Church, for which they also bear the responsibility.

The council also engages in a short reflection on the situation in the local churches by saying:

> Thanks to divine providence, the various churches which were established in various places by the Apostles and their successors have in the course of time coalesced into a number or organically connected communities. Without detriment to the unity of faith and the single divine constitution for the whole church, they enjoy their own discipline, their own liturgical usage, and their own theological and

spiritual heritage. Some of these churches, notably the ancient patriarchal churches, as parent-stocks of the faith, so to speak, have begotten other churches as daughter churches. With these they are connected down to our own time by close bonds of charity in their sacramental life, and in their mutual respect for rights and duties. This harmonious variety of local churches is particularly splendid evidence of the catholicity of the undivided Church. (No. 23)[80]

This refers to the churches of the East until the schism of 1054. But the fundamental structure of the Eastern church was not touched either, for it has survived to the present day. This structure is one reason why the Roman church never denied the churches of the East the designation "church," why Rome now offers eucharistic fellowship to the Eastern churches under certain conditions, and why the Eastern church is becoming the preferred partner in ecumenical dialogue with the Roman Catholic church.

Vatican II goes on to declare that the bishops, as total college in fellowship with the pope as head of the college, are teachers and witnesses of divine truth. If they unanimously present "a particular doctrine as binding, they proclaim in infallible fashion the teaching of Christ" (no. 25).[81]

Despite this description, Vatican II says more about the difference in tasks than about the superiority of bishops over presbyters. Presbyters and bishop together form one presbytery (no. 28); priests and bishops are united through ordination (ibid.). Priests represent the bishop in local parishes, and indeed render the whole church appropriately visible.[82]

This in fact points to great similarities between bishop and presbyter. The similarities do not exclude the differences in tasks, but do point to a relationship which binds them together. The Council of Trent explicitly rejected the view that the bishop is not the only legitimate dispenser of confirmation (DS 1630), but Vatican II speaks positively of the bishops as the first-called dispensers of confirmation (*ministri originarii*) (*Lumen Gentium*, no. 26).[83] Actually, confirmation is today administered by nonepiscopal officials too.

Could not what has been said and determined about confirmation also be said in principle about ordination, especially since there are historical models?[84] The coordination of both offices would thus be given prominence once again.

II

The question of the office of bishop has recurred repeatedly in the present ecumenical discussion regarding the ministerial office. The most recent documentation is the paper by the Roman Catholic–Lutheran Joint Commission on the topic of the ministerial office in the church, which is based on the document "The Gospel and the Church" (*Malta Paper*) and elaborates on it. Both documents contain reflections on the now-historical expansion of the one office in the church, and are indebted to this provenance. The document *The Ministry in the Church* states that the existence in both churches of local congregational offices and superior regional offices is not merely the result of purely human historical development or purely sociological necessity for both churches. Both churches consider it to be much more a work of the Spirit which the Church has experienced from the very beginning and to which it has testified. The development of the one ecclesiastical office into various offices can be comprehended as something more deeply related to the essence of the Church. The Church is embodied on several levels: as local church (congregation); as church of a larger district, such as territorial church; and as universal Church. It is essential on each of these levels that the ecclesiastical office remain, in ever-different ways, both in and over against the ecclesiastical community. Thus there is a notable structural parallelism between the two churches (no. 45).[85] "If both churches acknowledge that for faith this historical development of the one Apostolic Office into a more local and a more regional office has taken place with the help of the Holy Spirit, and to this degree constitutes something essential for the church, then a high degree of agreement has been reached" (no. 49).[86]

The World Council of Churches document of the Commission on Faith and Order, the *Lima Document* (1982), *Baptism, Eucharist, and Ministry*—the elaboration of the Accra document of the same title—explains, with regard to our topic:

> Today churches, including those engaged in union negotiations, are expressing willingness to accept episcopal succession as a sign of the apostolicity of the life of the whole Church. Yet at the same time, they cannot accept any suggestion that the ministerial office, exercised in

their own tradition, should be invalid until the moment that it enters into the existing line of episcopal succession. Their acceptance of the episcopal succession will best further the unity of the whole Church if it is part of a wider process by which the episcopal churches themselves also regain their lost unity. (No. 38)[87]

(Thesis VII will discuss the reservation "at the same time they cannot accept." This reservation must not render church unity impossible.)

III

Apostolic succession plays an important role in the texts we have discussed regarding the office of bishop.

For a long time, Catholics understood apostolic succession simply as merely the uninterrupted succession of bishops in the church. Thus when—as at the time of the Reformation—this chain was broken, apostolic succession appeared to be absolutely dissolved. There seemed to be a church-dividing disagreement on precisely this point. In the meantime, the thought that "the apostolic" and the apostolic succession are a part of the determination of the essence of the Church as a whole, and that apostolic succession means primarily something with regard to the contents, has gained more and more acceptance in all the churches. It means the succession of the whole Church in the apostolic faith.

Succession, in the sense of episcopal succession, should be seen in this overlapping aspect. The gospel's witness is tied to witnesses of the gospel. Therefore it can be said: Catholic doctrine understands the apostolic succession in the office of bishop to be sign of, and service to, the apostolicity of the church.

One can elaborate on this: the apostolic succession in the office of bishop is a *sign* of the apostolicity of the church, not apostolicity itself. Nor is it therefore an automatically effective guarantee. History demonstrates how bishops can fall out of the apostolic succession—for example, at the time of the Arian controversies, where it is not exactly certain that the majority of bishops represented correct teaching. This impression is strengthened when one considers the viewpoints and conditions under which bishops were appointed during the Middle Ages.

Moreover, it must be noted that it is hard to prove any uninterrupted historical continuity dating from the very beginning. Succession in the office of bishop is *one* sign of the apostolic succession, one sign among others. It is, however, an *essential sign* which, as the thesis states, must not be omitted in a one Church-to-be. (See Thesis VII.) A possible mutual recognition of offices must include this Catholic understanding of the ministerial office. The bishops, for their part, are bound to the canon of Scripture and to the apostolic tradition of faith, and must actively bear witness to them.[88] In the ecumenical discussion of today, "a high degree of agreement" is being reached through an identical emphasis on the fact that the understanding of apostolicity, with regard to content, is the primary one.

This is underlined by the fact that, for Lutheran tradition too, "the apostolic succession is necessary and constitutive for both the church and its ministerial office."[89] Thus the apostolic succession concentrated on the right proclamation of the gospel, which always included the ministerial office, "faith, and the witness of Christian life." This is the basis on which the ordination of ministers by ministers was performed in the Lutheran church. Thus the so-called presbyteral succession is considered not a substitute for, but a form of, episcopal succession, and leads to the following conclusion:

> In fact it is the Catholic conviction that standing in the historic succession belongs to the fullness of the episcopal office.
>
> But this fact does not, according to the Catholic view, preclude that the ministerial office in the Lutheran churches exercises essential functions of the office that Jesus Christ instituted in His Church.[90]

This assessment also throws light on how the frequently discussed phrase in the Vatican II *Decree on Ecumenism* (*Unitatis Redintegratio*, no. 22) regarding "deficiency of ordination (*defectus ordinis*)" should be understood.[91] The official translation, "due to the lack of sacrament of orders," which threatened to block ecumenical dialogue on the subject of ministerial office and ordination, has made room for a feasible new interpretation. "Defectus" need not mean total absence; it can also be understood as a deficiency of something which exists. In the document *The Ministry in the Church*, the suggested formulation is: "a deficiency of the fullness of the ecclesiastical office."[92] That is undoubtedly progress; but, on the basis of all that has been said, the text should have taken one further step, to the possibility of a recognition of ecclesiastical offices. This possibility is expressed as a wish (no. 81).[93]

As has been said, and will be said again, the answer to the retroactive question of validity or non-validity of ministerial offices in the churches of the Reformation (from the perspective of Catholics today) is not something that would have to block the future unity of the churches, even if the answers are different. But in any case, this is valid for the future: the churches are challenged, in the documents mentioned above, to test anew the possibility of reestablishing the connection with the historical succession of the office of bishop as sign of the unity of faith.

The Accra paper already pointed out—and the *Lima Document* reenforced—that the churches participating in union negotiations are willing to understand the office of bishop as a particularly important sign of the apostolic succession of the whole Church in faith, life, and doctrine. Thus they are willing to consider it something to strive for wherever it is lacking. The only thing they find irreconcilable with present historical and theological research is the notion that episcopal succession is simply identical with the apostolicity of the whole Church (no. 37).[94]

Edmund Schlink points out that the sequence of laying-on of hands is a sign of the apostolic succession of offices in the Church: that it points to the time-encompassing unity of the apostolic church. And because the laying-on of hands occurs with the assistance of shepherds of other congregations, it is a sign of the spatial extension of the one apostolic Church. What speaks on behalf of the bishop's laying-on of hands is "that this sequence is a clearer sign of the universal unity of the Church than is the sequence of local church ordinations. For the bishop is the bond of fellowship of many local churches. To that extent the sequence of laying-on of hands of bishops is to be preferred, and, where it is lacking, it should be strived for."[95]

It has become relatively apparent in the texts we have presented that there are positive conditions and starting points for the acceptance of the thesis, as well as a clearly recognizable willingness. The process has not yet ended; it must go on, and needs further communication and intensification.

IV

The question of episcopal election, viewed ecumenically—and therefore with a view to the one Church-to-be—is very important. It affects the range of the pope's universal jurisdictional primacy and its practical application, which is becoming effective in the partner churches and their subdivision.

According to the previous *Canon Law (Codex iuris canonici)* (can. 329), bishops are freely nominated by the pope.

In preparation of the filling of the bishop's office through the pope, a system of lists has been introduced everywhere, according to which the bishops of a country (in part by surveying trustworthy clerics or pastors) and sometimes the Cathedral chapters recommend qualified candidates to the Apostolic See, without placing any juridical obligation on him.[96]

A distinction is made between the system of relative lists, which is intended for a particular case to be settled, and the system of absolute lists, corresponding to lists to be submitted periodically to the apostolic see to inform him about qualified candidates for the episcopal office.

There are still exceptions to this rule in a few countries. There are elections of bishops through cathedral chapters, and—very rarely nowadays—presentations on the part of a national government. The free election of bishops by Cathedral chapters still occurs in the Swiss bishoprics of Basel, Chur, and St. Gallen, although the government has the right to appeal in these elections. The election is confirmed by the pope, which is meant to prove that investiture to the episcopal office is the responsibility of the pope. If for some reason the papal confirmation cannot occur, the cathedral chapter has the right to hold a new election.

In the Uniate Eastern churches, the bishop is elected by the synod of bishops of the patriarchate, under the chairmanship of the patriarch. That has been accepted in the so-called Eastern canon law, with the supplement, however, that the list of candidates must first be approved by Rome. Once concluded, the election does not need to be confirmed by the pope; he is merely to be informed of the result.

Vatican II took this situation into account when it explained "The canonical mission of bishops can come about by legitimate customs which have not been revoked by the supreme and universal authority of the church, by laws made or recognized by that same authority, or directly through the successor of Peter himself. In case he objects or denies the apostolic communion, the bishops cannot assume their office" (*Lumen Gentium*, no. 24).[97] The new *Canon Law*, can. 377 par. 1, states: "The Supreme Pontiff freely nominates a bishop or confirms his legitimate election (*episcopos libere nominat Summus Pontifex aut legitime electos confirmat*)." These texts once again make clear that there are various possible ways to elect or appoint a bishop, "and the only common element necessary to these various ways is that the bishop is accepted in the community of bishops which are represented by the Roman pope."[98]

A look at the history of the *election of bishops* and the filling of the office once again discloses a wide spectrum of possibilities.

A review of the history of the filling of offices in the early Church leaves no doubt that, with regard to bishops, an election by both laity and clerics was practiced from the very beginning. No matter how variable the forms of participation were, the role of the laity as a whole cannot be reduced to mere acclamation. This in no way means that an ecclesiastical office is conferred from below; rather, the work of the Holy Spirit is also expressed in the decision of the congregation.[99]

The episcopal office fell into a public conflict of interests at the time of state recognition of Christianity under Constantine (306–37), and the increasing integration of church and state. This conflict was not without consequences to the manner and method of appointing ecclesiastical officals. Ecclesiastical affairs assumed political importance, which led to governmental intervention. Yet the practice of electing the bishop through both laity and clergy was nevertheless maintained. Charlemagne claimed that his appropriation of the right to appoint bishops was the effluence of a power granted to him by God. The issue became even more complicated with the fusion of spiritual and secular affairs in the office of the bishop, since bishops were also bearers of secular authority. That is why kings, princes, and feudal lords sought to exert their power and influence in the election of bishops.

The eleventh-century reform movement, in the name of "freedom of the church (*libertas ecclesiae*)", demanded the return to the church of church investiture, particularly the free election of bishops by laity and clergy. Settlement of the investiture controversy signified the end of the so-called lay investiture, and the filling of ecclesiastical offices by ecclesiastial officials; in the case of elections of bishops, the election was held by the cathedral chapter. However, Pope Gregory VII, in particular, laid claim to the power of decision regarding the election of bishops. The right of confirmation was frequently used as a means to influence the election itself.[100]

Later developments regarding the election and appointment of bishops led to the right of feudal landlords to nominate and present candidates. However, these were rights which were viewed as papal privileges, and therefore as emanations of the papal right to install; these rights lapsed to a large extent, as a result of secularization, and required new arrangements which increasingly tended to favor papal appointment of bishops.

Vatican II dealt with this subject in the following way:

> The apostolic office of bishops was instituted by Christ the Lord, and serves a spiritual and supernatural purpose. The right of nominating and appointing bishops belongs properly, peculiarly, and of itself exclusively to the competent ecclesiastical authorities. Therefore, for the purpose of duly protecting the freedom of the church and of promoting more suitably and efficiently the welfare of the faithful, the Council desires that in the future no rights or privileges of election, nomination, presentation, or designation for the office of bishops be any longer granted to civil authorities.

Civil authorities are asked to renounce these rights and privileges voluntarily. (*Christus Dominus*, no. 20).[101]

Developments could also have taken another direction—if state intervention is to a large extent eliminated, then one of the most important reasons presented in favor of the practice of reserving to the Roman see the appointment of bishops is also eliminated. Another development would be contained in the intentions expressed in the Vatican II "*communio*" ecclesiology.

> The participation of all the people of God in the election of their bishops seems to be a requirement of the ecclesiology of community, which is gaining increasing acceptance and which has included several shifts of emphasis having far-reaching ecumenical consequences.[102]

One could draw the same conclusions from the fact that local churches received a higher revaluation at the Council. "The process of returning to local churches powers and rights which Rome had reserved to itself during the course of history must conclude with a return to them of the power to participate decisively in the election of their bishop."[103] This is not simply a concession to a concept of church, which is unjustly conceived of as a democracy; rather, it is an orientation to the church's origin, which in no way possesses a mere temporal significance.

It must be added that these determinations in the new *Canon Law* are being actuated, and, with regard to our topic of episcopal election, this is being done in the direction of a greater degree of openness. This openness is also, and in particular, an effect of what was said at Vatican II about bishops and episcopal office. This openness creates additional feasibility for our thesis that all partner churches, in accordance with ancient tradition, have bishops at the head of their larger subdivisions.

THESIS VI

The partner churches live in mutual fraternal exchange of all aspects of their life, so that the previous history and experience of the churches separated earlier can become effective in the life of the other partner churches.

This thesis corresponds to the perceived goal of the one Church-to-be, which is to be understood not as a Church of uniformity, but rather as a unity in variety, as conciliar fellowship, as Church of reconciled diversity. The precondition for such a goal is the mutual recognition which itself presupposes mutuality and diversity.

I

This thesis is directed against various other tendencies. First, against the tendency to see and evaluate the previous history and experience of the still-separated churches in *solely* negative terms. It is true that the separation of the churches should not exist, and that this separation depicts guilt and trouble, but we will not do justice to these facts, either in general or in detail, if we use these categories alone.

Whoever sees only the negative side will also consider past experience and history only an expression and a form of being separated. At the same time, they will use it as a means of asserting, reenforcing, and solidifying separation. From this perspective, the other person or thing is the alien and the enemy.

The partner churches define themselves by their respective contrast to the other. Thus being Catholic means not being Protestant, and vice versa. Negation becomes one element in the strengthening of one's own community. With this kind of negative fundamental choice and attitude, one sees everything differently—and one sees it negatively. Defects of the other churches are noticed with a certain amount of gratification when one has this attitude. One also hopes silently *tacitly* that, as a result of these defects, the other church will soon dissolve on its own. And one adds that the dissolution of the other will work in favor of one's own partner church which would gain from, and be strengthened by, the breakup of the other.

This viewpoint denies the indisputable fact that an unmistakable community—more basic than any differences—exists between the confessional churches. It denies the fact of a common heritage and long common history, starting with the apostolic origins testified to in the Bible. During the preceding history of one thousand years, the Christian Church—with the exception of a few clusters and splinter groups—presented, despite all its variety, the history and experience of a single unit. This viewpoint denies the fact that what really should not be—the schism of the Church—has in the course of history received an independent shape of its own, which one cannot in any way assess in just negative terms. No life can grow, and no permanence can result, from bare negation.

Although what was done cannot be undone, what was done can, in the course of history, be changed and transformed; it can emerge from simple antithesis and attain its own positive value.

Our thesis presupposes that there is diversity between the partner churches: diversity in the forms of faith, of piety, of liturgy, of theology, of spirituality, of traditions, of life styles, of practice, of external symbols, of nontheological factors, and of attention to the world. At the same time, this thesis assumes that these historical experiences have lost their church-dividing character and can become a reconciled diversity—not as a result of an artificial metamorphosis, but as a result of the insight that they are various forms of expression within a communality. They have lost their "anti" character and gained a positive independence.

Our thesis furthermore presupposes, and includes, the fact that past history and experience of the still-separated churches is tolerable. It is not tolerable simply because of possible reversion to a common foundation, but because of the recognition, insight, and experience that a large amount of tolerance and freedom must be granted to matters of church practice, piety, jurisprudence, liturgy, spirituality, and theology; and that the thought of diversity in unity has its rights here, if anywhere. This is already apparent in the form of the Eastern churches united with Rome. It is apparent in the important offer of freedom to the Orthodox churches—to their independent history and experience, which are to be preserved in the one Church-to-be, and indeed, the protection of which is one of the duties of a Petrine service in the Church.

Nevertheless, merely tolerating the other would not be enough, and would still be burdened by the shadow of negativeness or of the not very pleasant. The history and experience of the still-separated partner churches can be communicated, can be shared, and can be exchanged. They take place in a mutual give-and-take which leads to a fraternal exchange. This does not mean that one's own tradition is lifted, in the sense of being eliminated; rather, it is lifted, in the sense of being preserved, and in the sense of being enhanced. One's own tradition and experience is enriched and becomes greater and more intensive than it was before.

At the present time such an exchange in the churches can be clearly recorded. The Catholic church—long viewed as the church of sacraments, in contradistinction to the Protestant church, which was considered the church of the word—by its intensive attention to the Word of God in its various forms of revelation of God, Word of God in written form in the Bible, and Word of God in proclamation, has let itself be enriched by the Protestant church. Nor can there be any doubt that, as a result of this fraternal exchange, the Protestant church has found new access to the actuality of the sacraments, above all to the Eucharist. The Catholic church has concerned itself intensively with the theology of the cross and the doctrine of the hidden God, particularly prominent in the Protestant church. The Protestant church has opened itself anew to a theology of creation and of earthly realities.

One can, of course, say that all the contents now being presented as exchange and enrichment really existed already in the separated partner churches in principle. But their actual and intensive realization is a result of fraternal exchange. Their realization would not have become effective in this manner without this exchange.

This fraternal exchange is commanded today in particular. It is far removed from satisfaction at the misfortune, failure, or deficiencies of the other partner churches, and from the totally false expectation that their downfall helps one's own growth and expansion. Today it is not the individual confessions but Christian existence itself, faith in God, which is called into question and challenged by secularism, atheism, and criticism of religion. It is not the individual confessions but the Christian faith itself which is being asked whether the confessions can be an authority capable of establishing and imparting meaning to life and death.

Not individual churches but the churches collectively are being asked what contributions they have the power to make toward serving justice and peace; toward resisting violence, terror, and suppression; toward promoting human dignity, human rights, and basic ethical values as the irrevocable foundation for a society. The churches collectively are being asked for responsibility toward the world; above all they are being asked for an ethical orientation, derived from themselves, through which the current problems can be solved successfully: may one—responsibly—do what one is technologically capable of doing? How do we acquire moral power over the technological powers?

What ensues is that no one confession alone can respond effectively to this universal challenge aimed at the very core. This is where the combined experience and history of the churches must be called into service, for together they can accomplish more than one partner church alone. As a result, it becomes clear that the diversity of history and experience in the partner churches can also be an advantage, and that the otherness of the other need not be experienced as alien or hostile, but rather as merit: "it is good that you are there; my own becomes richer through you; I would be poorer without you." That is how the fear of contact is overcome. Like all fear, this one is a poor counselor.

A new tradition is established in the partner churches through this demand and its inherent challenge, and through the fraternal exchange becoming effective therein; indeed, a new and greater *identity* is forged. If for a long time it was believed that one's own identity could only be achieved by mutual delimitations, then the new identity is based on the communality achieved in fraternal exchange. One's own is not destroyed thereby; instead, it is in a positive sense "lifted"—preserved, elevated, and brought into a larger context.

Every partner church claims to be essentially catholic—catholic in the sense of the Apostolic Creed, even when "Christian" or "universal" is said instead of catholic. But catholicity, including that of the Roman Catholic church, is diminished by the fact of the separation of the churches. That is a declaration by Vatican II. The increasingly effective fraternal exchange in the partner churches is an expression of the greater and more intensive catholicity—expression and form of Christ's treasures—and a sign of the many gifts of the Spirit which works many charisms and which blows when, where, and how it wills.

This insight must become even more manifest in concrete reality. This means that there is not just the task of guarding and protecting the homogeneity of confessional interior space. (This intention finds expression in many actual church directives such as those regarding ecumenical Sunday worship service, the exclusion of mixed-marriage couples from service in the church, the intensification of the confessional principle in catechism.) Meanwhile, the fraternal exchange which has become a reality and which today shapes and determines the churches decisively, must not be overlooked; experiences of fellowship must achieve even more intensive and tangible forms of actualization. For instance, it must be admitted that a mixed marriage can also be a place of real ecumenicity. Moreover, much more is possible today than is actually being done; we are permitted more than we are able to do.

The growing fraternal exchange could be as enriching to the Church as that between Jewish Christians and Gentile Christians at the time of the Church's beginning; or as the fraternal exchange with the churches of the East, from whom no one demands the sacrifice of their history and experience. Indeed everyone wishes they would preserve both and bring them into the variety in unity, into reconciled diversity, into the larger catholicity. Similar things could be said about the fraternal exchange of the churches on the various continents with their different traditions and acculturations.

The Roman Catholic church has had a long experience in rehearsing for unity. Often, especially after Vatican I, it has understood this unity as uniformity, and has articulated it in delimitation from other churches and confessions. It must now rehearse a process which understands unity not as monolithic unity but as a unity of which the expression—not the antithesis—is living diversity.

The non–Roman Catholic churches, especially the churches of the Reformation, have a long experience in what diversity means, including its inherent danger of splintering. They have a need to catch up in the rehearsing for unity in the midst of diversity. Mutual fraternal exchange in all aspects of life does not bring loss but enrichment; it endangers neither tradition nor identity, but instead lends it a more intensive, greater, and more effective form.

II

Our thesis is also directed against a very different tendency. There are voices today pleading for a transformation of confessional identity. They insist that the specifically confessional "I" must die, so that the ecumenical Christ and an ecumenical Christianity may gain shape. The reasoning is that whatever is specific to a confession originated in the principle of opposites as a result of delimitation, and thus inhibits ecumenicity—in factual terms, the one Church-to-be. Therefore clinging to confessional identities would be irresponsible and indeed would spread the sin of separation.[104]

In opposition to this, it must be asserted that confessional specificity is in no way a clearly determined and unequivocal entity. Furthermore, it did not originate as only delimitation and defense against "the other"—therefore in the principle of opposites. It can also have grown in the soil of a great communality through a particular emphasis. This becomes quite evident with regard to the Orthodox church, but is also applies in large measure to the church of the Reformation, which, as is well known, did not just begin in the sixteenth century. Nor can the Catholic church since then be described solely in terms of the Counter-Reformation.

The demand to transform confessional identity by eliminating confessional specificity could look like the creation of a third confession, which would not eliminate the separation, but instead increase it by one more. Besides, ecumenical Christianity so understood would be in danger of becoming an abstract entity which could not actually be lived. Or a new form of ecumenical united Church could result, which would not be protected against the danger of uniformity and the monolithic, but which would instead only be given a new shape.

The elimination of confessional specificity—in other words, the demolition of the respective confessional outlines—might drive those at home in the confessions into homelessness. That in turn would be a loss, including a loss to ecumenicity. All of this can also be formulated in this way: ecumenicity must not substitute for the confessions; rather, the confessions should be form and expression of ecumenicity. Loyalty to one's own can most certainly be combined with ecumenical openness; churches should remain churches *and* become one Church (Ratzinger).

In other words, this means that confessional specificity should not simply be eliminated, nor should it lose its outline and become a mere shadow of itself. It should be recognizable—in the sense of a reconciled diversity—on the strength of a tolerance which arises from faith and which has the strength to endure. For example: it should not be a matter of eliminating what is specifically Catholic— veneration of Mary, eucharistic piety, Corpus Christi processions, pilgrimages, the rosary, genuflecting, the sign of the cross. Rather, these things should be preserved, and renewed where it seems advisable; and their anti-Reformation accent should be removed, which has happened in several places with respect to the practice of Corpus Christi processions. What is required is not abolition but recognition and reconciliation.

Yet no one demands that one partner church simply take on the specifically confessional practice of the other churches; nor are they required to do so for the sake of ecumenicity. But what is required is that the confessional specificity in the practice of one confession is acknowledged as not being contrary to the gospel and that therefore it must not be condemned or rejected. Moreover, it could be viewed as a possible development of the Christian faith. The notion which was once expressed, that ecumenicity would be achieved when Catholics and Protestants pray the rosary together before the displayed monstrance is absurd. Such a requirement cannot even be made specifically confessional—thus making it binding on all Catholics—much less a condition for, or expression of, ecumenicity.

If our thesis is accepted, it will guard against the danger of thinking that one can only realize one's own at the expense of the other. Tied to that notion is the belief that the other must supply the dark background so that one's own can be more luminously presented. What is Christian and catholic does not live by making others small or bad or despicable. Rather, it has the strength of a universal recognition: it is great by perceiving the other as great too.

If our thesis is accepted and realized, it will demolish the fear that the model of the prodigal son will be used in the concept of the ecumenical goal. The fear of a takeover or unconditional surrender will also be demolished. It is time to part with these models. Our thesis is equally qualified to remove from Christians living in, and at home in, the confessions their fear of a loss of identity and continuity. We should become convinced that we shall not get poorer but richer; we shall not lose catholicity, we shall add a new dimension. We shall not be deprived of what we can cling to, we shall gain even more support and guidance. Loyalty to one's own does not exclude, it includes openness toward the other. And openness toward the other can be openness toward something greater. Indeed, it may even mean a greater loyalty to one's own.

It is impossible to list all the individual areas of such collaboration between the partner churches. Some examples: the works of charity (*Diakonie*) and *Caritas*; the projects of "Misereor" and "Bread for the World"; adult education; Bible study; ecumenical workshops; ministry to the sick and telephone ministry; commitment to social action; joint championing of basic human rights, justice, and peace. There is already quite a bit of collaboration among the churches in these areas. But this collaboration could be much greater and much less inhibited if the churches already lived in the one Church.

THESIS VII

Without prejudice to the judgment of another church concerning the theological legitimacy of the existing ministerial office in the separated churches, all partner churches commit themselves henceforth to conduct ordinations with prayer and the laying-on of hands, so that acknowledging them will present no difficulty for the Roman Catholic partner church either.

For the sake of the unity of the Church, Thesis VII attempts to deal with a subject which is one of the most difficult problems discussed in ecumenical dialogues: the mutual *recognition of ministerial offices*. There is no controversy on this issue between the churches of the East and the Latin church, since the difficulty between them is not a sacramental but merely a juridical one. One could point out that the Latin church recognizes the validity of the absolution in the Eastern church's sacrament of penance (which may be rather important to the issue of ecumenicity in the West). However, this is not merely a purely sacramental matter, but also a juridical question pertaining to so-called jurisdiction, according to the teaching of the Council of Trent. Thus what is being recognized in this case is also an effectively valid juridical power in churches separated from Rome.

The whole issue of ministerial offices is a much more difficult one in the relationship between the Roman church and the churches of the Reformation. It is almost self-evident that the large *churches of the Reformation* insist that they have not only baptized validly up to now, but that they also celebrate the Lord's Supper with effectiveness and validity. (No one denies this although, ever since the time of Cyprian, the question has really never been answered as to how there could be effective sacramental procedures outside the Catholic church; and conversely, if there could be, why no other sacraments beyond that of baptism are accepted, and therefore why other sacraments cannot also be valid outside the Catholic church—unless one thinks in absolutely positivistic terms, and then cannot explain how one knows this positive positioning of God.)

But the Roman Catholic church contests (except in special cases) the validity of ordination (of priest and bishops) which is the necessary precondition for celebrating the Lord's Supper. Therefore it refuses to grant the Lord's Supper in the Reformation churches the same sacramental dignity possessed by the Catholic mass. The question, therefore, becomes critical with respect to sacramental validity of ordination.

As far as the Anglican orders are concerned, Leo XIII did declare them "invalid," referring to the fact that the "intention" necessary to the validity of ordination had not existed at the beginning of the separated Anglican church, and that this lack rendered later ordinations invalid as well. But this doctrine of Leo XIII is controversial even within the Catholic church itself. There are serious theological studies concluding that, according to its own doctrine of sacraments, the Catholic church may not reject the validity of Anglican ordinations because a theoretical error in the understanding of a sacramental act does not abrogate its actual validity or the necessary "intention." Therefore, by revising the doctrine of Leo XIII—which is not impossible—one could come to a relatively easy agreement with the Anglicans about the validity of their orders and of the sacramental acts based on them, as far as the past is concerned.

The prevailing understanding of sacramental ordination in the Catholic church makes it much more difficult for that church to recognize the validity of ordination in the other Reformation churches, even if it is done with prayer and the laying-on of hands. It is said that the ministers in these churches were, at the outset, not installed through the *bishops's* laying-on of hands, and therefore these ordinations were invalid then and remained invalid later, which resulted in the Catholic judgment regarding the Protestant Lord's Supper. It must be admitted that the Catholic church considers this interpretation of ordination in the Protestant churches to be more or less unequivocal and definite. Thus it cannot be expected, in the foreseeable future, that Rome and the Catholic bishops will renounce this—albeit not definitive—doctrine and the conclusions usually drawn from it. (See Thesis V.)

However, it may be added that this prevailing Catholic interpretation of ordination in the Protestant churches is being challenged. After all, it is not simply self-evident why their faithfully given testimony to Christ's grace should not be valid sacraments, at a time when these other Christian churches exist in an undisputed state of security regarding their self-understanding. But be that as it may, under the given circumstances—which cannot really be overcome in the foreseeable future—an agreement on the validity or nonvalidity of *past* ordination in the Reformation churches cannot really be expected to occur between the Reformation churches and the Roman Catholic church.

But it can and should be noted, first of all, that it is uncertain that this dissension about the past means controversy regarding more secure "dogmas" on either side. In conformity with Thesis II one can, to this extent, drop this dissension at the time of unification without exacting from either side an absolute interpretation of these past ordinations which would be perceived as correct by the other side. Moreover, it is clear, even according to the conventional Catholic doctrine on grace and sacraments—for example, with reference to the Tridentine doctrine—that the true body and blood of Jesus Christ can also be received through a "spiritual" communion (DS 1648) independent of the eucharistic signs, as long as they are simply acknowledged as valid. Nor need the truly grace-filled effects of the "rites" in the Reformation churches be denied, even when, in conformity to this conventional doctrine, the attribute "sacrament" is denied them; which probably makes it a matter not just of the subject itself, but also in part of a mere linguistic arrangement.

If, at the time of unification, one drops the issue of the past—and both sides, in the final analysis, are also permitted to drop it, according to our theses—then the only issue is what the *present and future* attitude should be with regard to ordination, so that a mutual recognition of the ministerial offices is possible. This issue must be divided into several questions.

First of all, the question is *which* offices and installations into office must be designated sacramental acts in all the churches which are uniting, and whether these offices and their ranking should be the same in all partner churches. As far as the office of bishop is concerned, all the necessary things about it and about its existence in all partner churches have already been said in the Commentary to Thesis V. The issue here is therefore the other offices.

In this connection it must first be emphasized that there is not the unequivocal and total clarity in the present Catholic doctrine on offices by divine right (*iuris divini*) that one often silently assumes it to be in ecumenical discussions. The more or less general teaching is that, obviously, the office of bishop, the simple priesthood, and the diaconate have been offices by divine law (*iuris divini*) from the very beginning of the Church. But there is no total clarity or agreement in present Catholic theology regarding the manner in which these offices, in their three-tiered ranking, can be (must be?) traced back to Jesus Christ. If these three offices are interpreted to be by divine law (*ius divinum*), then such a doctrine is quite compatible with the assumption that the division into these three offices of the ultimately single and necessary office in the Church was undertaken in an irreversible manner in apostolic times. Nor did it have to be based on an explicit command of Jesus or of one of the apostles.

For the sake of future unity, one will be able to say that when (in accordance with Thesis V) all churches have bishops, none of the partner churches will find it difficult to have leaders officially commissioned by the Church who celebrate the Eucharist and give absolution, who are not bishops but who are members and assistants. Thus there will be officials in all the churches whom we call "priests" in the Catholic sense.

The more difficult question probably is whether there will have to be "deacons," in the sense of the Orthodox and the Latin churches, in the non–Roman Catholic partner churches of the one Church everywhere, who are differentiated from other official coworkers in the Church. If one remembers that for centuries there were really no deacons in the Latin church (or rather, that they led a rather fictitious life) and that the diaconate was in fact considered merely a ritual transitional level leading to priesthood; if one further remembers that lower orders (of subdeacon, etc.) were considered sacramental orders in medieval theology up to and including the Council of Florence—that therefore the church was essentially granted a lot of leeway in the division of its one office—then one will have to be cautious in answering the question whether in future the diaconate must exist in every partner church in exactly the same way as in the Roman Catholic partner church.

In order to accomplish the variety of tasks, there could perhaps be several ecclesiastical offices under and beside the priestly office, in a variety of arrangements in the partner churches, appropriate to their respective traditions. None of them needs to be an exact copy of the Roman and Eastern churches' diaconates. (Particularly since there is less than great clarity in the determination of the content of this diaconate in both the East and in the Latin church. Thus it is rather certain that the same name was applied to relatively different offices in these churches at various times.)

Under these circumstances, a considerable amount of leeway can be granted the non-Latin partner churches in dividing the ultimately single office in the Church below the "priesthood." If they do have any ecclesiastical offices under and beside the offices of bishop and priest at all, which is probably to be expected when judged by the objective necessities of church life, then the office nearest that of priest in its duties could be called "diaconate" without reservation. Roman Catholics could rate it equal to their diaconate, so that the division into three offices (besides the many others which exist everywhere, at least with respect to human and historically variable law) should not really need to present insurmountable obstacles to unity.

A further question is how these offices in the one Church should be transmitted, so that every partner church can recognize the legitimacy of the transmission of the office in the other partner churches.

There is probably no basic difficulty between the partner churches on the point that, in future, the ordination of bishops and priests will occur in all partner churches through prayer and the laying-on of hands. Since the Catholic church has no dogmatically binding way to confer the office of those the Catholics call "deacons," no insurmountable difficulty should arise between the partner churches with regard to such a rite either.

The more difficult question concerns the Roman Catholic understanding of the transmission of office (for bishops and priests): in the partner churches of the Reformation uniting with Rome, are there officials qualified to do the future laying-on of hands with sacramental authority, through which new bishops and priests are commissioned? According to the doctrine prevalent in the Roman Catholic church, the leading officials in the Protestant churches (except for exceptional cases) do not possess this sacramental authority, and therefore cannot "validly ordain."

In order to eliminate this problem for Catholic understanding of ordination, one could immediately suggest—if only to make visible faithful and loving unity among the partner churches—that episcopal representatives of the Roman partner churches participate in future ordinations in the Reformation partner churches, since an ordination through the laying-on of hands by several bishops is no liturgical problem. In cases like this, which the Reformation partner churches could readily permit, the Roman Catholics would no longer have any reservations concerning the validity of that ordination. If, in some cases, such a transmission of office, valid by even the most severe Roman Catholic standards, failed to occur because no bishop— reliably and validly ordained according to Roman Catholic theology—had participated (as with already-ordained pastors) or would participate, one could nevertheless let it pass. Only in a few individual cases would a situation continue that had existed before unification. Moreover, that situation (seen from the perspective of Roman Catholic theology) would disappear slowly but surely if, in many cases of new ordination, the participation of a bishop validly ordained by Roman Catholic principles would be admitted.

If a Roman Catholic theologian were not disposed to tolerate such an understanding and such a temporary practice of ordination, he would have to be asked how he can really explain the reliable validity of ordination in the existing Roman Catholic church. He cannot simply claim that the sacramental succession in ordination has never been interrupted (either through the lack of real intention or of other conditions normally required for validity). In cases like these, which cannot be ruled out, every Catholic theologian must assume that these ordinations are nevertheless valid because they are recognized as valid without challenge in the one Church, which is always sacramentally effective.

Why may something similar not be assumed in the cases under discussion? Ordinations are ultimately valid not because it is absolutely certain that, even in exceptional cases, they have corresponded to the concept of an almost physical norm of effectiveness of the sacraments (which in normal cases ordinations *should*, of course). They are valid because they are deemed valid within the one Church, and because they must be acknowledged as valid in a variety of situations.

There are analogous cases pertaining to marriage: can one seriously rate a marriage "invalid" before God, when there was a "procedural error," for which no one was seriously to blame and which was entirely unavoidable under the actual circumstances? Or can one say that such a marriage is valid even with *that kind* of procedural error, because it is nevertheless a reality in the church and is lived in this church as a Christian marriage?

THESIS VIII

There is pulpit and altar fellowship between the individual partner churches.

I

It has always been considered a rupture of the unity of faith and of the Church to set altar against altar, to deny or exclude someone from sacramental fellowship (*communio*) in the Lord's Supper. It is excommunication (*excommunicacio*) in the truest and deepest sense of the word. At the same time, it is the most severe contradiction to the Eucharist itself, which from the very beginning had been regarded as sign of unity and as basis of church community, corresponding to the Pauline declaration, "The cup of blessing which we bless, is it not a participation in the blood of Christ? The bread which we break, is it not a participation in the body of Christ? Because there is *one* bread, we who are many are *one* body, for we all partake of the one bread" (1 Cor. 10:16–17).

Church fellowship presents itself as *eucharistic fellowship*: the body of Christ (the Church) subsists on the body of Christ (the Eucharist). Broken church fellowship manifests itself as broken eucharistic fellowship; broken eucharistic fellowship denotes and effects broken church fellowship.

Thus it follows that as long as no eucharistic fellowship exists there will be no church fellowship, and as long as no church fellowship exists, there will be no eucharistic fellowship. Eucharistic fellowship is realization of church fellowship. Here is an insoluble interior connection and, at the same time, a circulation of what is alive and what stakes everything to penetrate this connection.

This state of affairs finds expression in the two formulations: "The Eucharistic fellowship demands and furthers the actual community of faith within the church";[105] or "The Eucharistic fellowship is expression and sign of church fellowship, but Eucharist and Eucharistic fellowship are also a way of achieving church fellowship."

These statements were also formulated in the texts of Vatican II, although they were not integrated. The council speaks of two principles: "The signifying of the unity of the church and the sharing in the means of grace. The signifying of unity generally rules out fellowship in worship, yet concern for grace sometimes recommends it."[106]

The way this issue is handled in *present practice* and thought, especially on the part of the Roman Catholic church, is to declare that eucharistic fellowship is the expression of church fellowship and fellowship of faith, the climax and culmination of ecumenical paths, as it were. However, it is said, since unity in faith has not yet been attained in full measure, eucharistic fellowship is not yet possible; it would be a concealment of ecclesiological reality, and a pretense of a state of affairs which does not yet exist. Furthermore, separation at the Lord's Supper should be borne for the sake of truth and honesty; for healing's sake, the wound thus exposed should not be closed too soon. It is also said that the admitted scandal here revealed of the most profound separation of the churches in the communion in the sacramental body of the Lord—which should really bind them together—should be borne for the sake of truth; for there could be no unity at the expense of truth. The sting contained in this, however, is an ever-new reason to work and to pray for unity in faith, so that eucharistic fellowship can occur.

That is the meaning of the Vatican II statement: "The unity of believers, who form one body in Christ, is expressed and realized through the sacrament of Eucharistic bread (1 Cor. 10:17). All human beings are called to this union with Christ, who is the Light of the world: we come from Him, we live through Him, we strive towards Him" (*Lumen Gentium*, no. 3).[107]

All churches are in agreement regarding the affirmation of this goal; this applies especially to the more recent statements of the World Council of Churches, which describes the goal of church fellowship to be that all Christians can visibly and together celebrate the Lord's Supper. This was their most recent statement issued at the assembly in Nairobi.

The document *Ways to Community* states:

We are saddened that the present relationship of our churches do not yet allow full Eucharistic fellowship. We confess anew our longing for "the goal of visible unity in one faith and in one Eucharistic fellowship." The credibility of our witness to the world and of our very celebrations of the Eucharist is menaced by our divisions at these celebrations. This suggests that the work of the Holy Spirit is not absent from the great pressure for Eucharistic fellowship we are now experiencing. We shall not cease to search for possible ways to allow mutual admission to communion in special cases. (No. 81)[108]

The thesis presented here presupposes, and accepts, the conception that altar and pulpit fellowship is expression and goal of a community in faith, and that, on the other hand, altar and pulpit fellowship is possible and indeed required, if the conditions for making it possible are present. The question is whether and how such a community in faith can occur, be produced, or be usefully established.

That pulpit fellowship is added to altar fellowship is based on the recognition that, even by present Catholic opinion, the complete form of a worship service is celebration of both Word and meal. A Catholic eucharistic celebration, especially on Sundays, is incomplete without a service of the Word in reading, proclamation, and confession. No less problematic is the practice in Protestant churches of a mere service of the Word—perhaps even as the regular form—or a "worship service with Lord's Supper." This distinction leads to the notion that the Eucharist is a supplement to the worship service and could be separated from the real worship service- —possibly even by distributing the communion in the sacristy.

Pulpit fellowship is already being practiced in many cases; and it no longer presents a disquieting exception, even to Catholic Christians. But one really should think about this more than ever, since it is precisely a pulpit fellowship which presupposes a community of faith. Consider the reality of salvation of the Word of God; consider Christ's presence in its various forms, including the form of proclamation; finally, consider the theological conformity of Word and Sacrament—sacrament as visible Word (*verbum visibile*), the Word as audible sacrament (*sacramentum audibile*).[109]

One could behold an even greater convergence between the churches in the fact that—without detriment to the thesis that the Eucharist is the source, center, and climax of the Church's life and thus depicts the climax of the worship service in the life of the congregation—a service of the Word, without celebration of the Eucharist, is held in a few congregations as a result of the scarcity of priests. It counts as fulfillment of the Sunday duty imposed on Catholics. Vivid words are used in these services to point to the presence of Christ in the Word of Scripture readings and in the Word of proclamation.

Pulpit and altar fellowship is also both the consequence and the form of the unity achieved in the "Leuenberg Concord (*Konkordie*)" between Evangelical-Lutheran and Reformed churches.[110] Unity was held to be feasible when they became convinced that the mutual condemnations of earlier days—precisely on the issue of Lord's Supper— —did not apply to today's altered circumstances.

A similar process and procedure of reassessment is also indicated, and imperative, in the relationship of the Roman Catholic church to the churches of the Reformation. It is equally remarkable and salutary that an intensive theological attempt to address this task is being undertaken between Catholic and Protestant theologians and, as far as can be determined so far, is being done with complete confidence.

II

Let us repeat the conditions for a possible pulpit and altar fellowship:

(a) The already-existing fellowship among Christians is a foundation. The baptism performed in the Christian churches with water and in the name of the triune God is recognized as valid sacrament in all Christian churches. Baptism signifies and effects the believers' bond to the life, death, and resurrection of the Lord (Rom. 6:4). Christians are conformed to Christ through baptism. "For we are all baptized in the one Spirit, into the one body of the Lord" (1 Cor. 12:13) (*Lumen Gentium*, no. 7).[111] "Incorporated into the Church through baptism, the faithful are consecrated by the indelible character to the exercise of the Christian religion. Reborn as sons of God, they must confess before humanity the faith which they have received from God through the Church" (*Lumen Gentium*, no. 11).[112]

The most important text is in the *Decree on Ecumenism* (*Unitatis Redintegratio*, no. 22):[113]

By the sacrament of baptism, whenever it is properly conferred in the way the Lord determined, and received with the appropriate dispositions of soul, a human being becomes truly incorporated into the crucified and glorified Christ and is reborn to a sharing of the divine life, as the apostle says, "for you were buried together with Him in baptism,

126

and in Him also rose again through faith in the working of God, who raised Him from the dead." (Col. 2:12; cf. Rom. 6:4)

Baptism, therefore, constitutes a sacramental bond of unity linking all who have been reborn by means of it. But baptism, of itself, is only a beginning, a point of departure, for it is wholly directed toward the acquiring of fullness of life in Christ. Baptism is thus oriented toward a complete profession of faith, a complete incorporation into the system of salvation such as Christ Himself willed it to be, and finally, toward a complete participation in eucharistic communion.

There is no doubt that a fundamental unity of Christians is being expressed here. It follows from the principle that Christians who are conformed to Christ—His person, His death, and His resurrection—thereby have a fellowship with each other; they are connected through a sacramental bond. And this unity is fundamental, even if not yet complete. That is demonstrated by the indication to the eucharistic fellowship, on which the community grounded in baptism is centered.

(b) But even with regard to *Eucharist* and *Lord's Supper*, there already are, between the churches, not only differences but common interests, which form an important basis for pulpit and altar fellowship.

As far as the Roman Catholic church is concerned, eucharistic fellowship with the Orthodox churches is already feasible under certain circumstances, as a result of the Orthodox understanding of Eucharist. Furthermore, the Roman Catholic church recognizes the Orthodox ordinations, in connection with the apostolic tradition and succession represented in the episcopal office.

In the Vatican II church constitution, the segment dealing specifically with the Christians of other churches states that they receive the sign of baptism, which binds them to Christ; "indeed, they also recognize and receive other sacraments within their own churches or ecclesiastical communities (*imo et alia sacramenta in propriis ecclesiis vel communitatibus ecclesiasticis agnoscunt et recipiunt*)" (*Lumen Gentium*, no. 15).[114] That "Eucharist" is meant by "other sacraments" follows from the context which states, without distinguishing "churches or ecclesial communities" that they recognize "other sacraments," the reception of which is "confirmed" by Catholics. In the Reformation churches it is the Lord's Supper in particular. If one had wanted to except the Reformation churches from this fundamental discussion from the very beginning, one could have set a limitation to that effect.

This positive eligibility of the sacraments is retained in the depiction of the Reformation churches, albeit with some reservations because of the "deficiency of the sacrament of ordination (*defectus sacramenti ordinis*)." It is retained to the extent that the *Decree on Ecumenism* (*Unitatis Redintegratio*, no. 22) declares that when they commemorate the death and resurrection of the Lord in the Lord's Supper, they confess that this designates the living fellowship with Christ, and that His glorious return is expected.[115] To judge by the intention of those who celebrate, this does not differ from the congregations' collective call of proclamation in the Catholic worship service, which follows the proclamation of the words of institution, "We proclaim your death, oh Lord, and we praise your resurrection until you come in glory."

Thus the intended meaning and content of the Lord's Supper are identical in both churches. However, the almost universal Catholic opinion doubts whether the intended content and meaning are fully achieved in the Protestant Lord's Supper, because of the "deficiency of ordination (*defectus ordinis*)." In any case, the original formulation of no. 22 (which Paul VI revised without necessarily altering its meaning) only said that the "full reality (*plena realitas*)" of the Lord's Supper was lacking. If one adds the doctrine of Trent (DS 1648) on the ("merely") spiritual but real reception of the "heavenly bread," then—even by assuming the just-mentioned Catholic opinion—one can say that what is present in the existing Protestant Lord's Supper is a deficiency in the sacramental sign, not a deficiency in the designated matter.

These reflections are important to the issue because they demonstrate that an altar fellowship is feasible as soon as there is sufficient unity of faith and as soon as the churches have become partner churches of the one Church, even if they continue to exist as partner churches (with their own liturgy, etc.).

Extensive agreement has been achieved in the ecumenical dialogue regarding the previously controversial issue of the *Lord's Supper as sacrifice*, as representation of the crucifixion—therefore the sacrifice of Jesus (in sacramental presence)—and of the possible sacrifice of the church, if this is understood to mean that the church has been taken into the self-offering of Jesus Christ and allows itself to be taken into the one consummation of self-offering. Above all, the abolition of misleading formulations was achieved.[116]

The document of the Roman Catholic–Lutheran Joint Commission regarding the Eucharist demonstrates impressively:

> The members of the body of Christ are united through Christ with God and with one another in such a way that they become participants in His worship, His self-offering, His sacrifice to the Father. Through this union between Christ and Christians, the Eucharistic assembly "offers Christ" by consenting in the power of the Holy Spirit to be offered by Him to the Father. Apart from Christ, we have no gifts, no worship, no sacrifice of our own to offer to God. All we can plead is Christ, the sacrificial Lamb and Victim whom the Father Himself has given us. (No. 58)[117]

(c) Thesis I dealt with the *community of faith*, stated as precondition for a possible pulpit and altar fellowship (beyond a common understanding of baptism and Lord's Supper). It is a unity regarding the fundamental truths of Christianity as they are expressed in Holy Scripture, in the Apostles' Creed, and in the Creed of Nicaea and Constantinople. The creeds are both the concentrated testimony of Holy Scripture and its normative interpretation. They are the common confession of the not-yet-separated churches of East and West—the year 1981 produced an agreement on this point from all the churches. They are the constitutive element of worship services in all the churches, especially in connection with the celebration of the Lord's Supper—which is constituted in Word and sacrament. This creates a commonality of the Church in space and time, in both synchronic and diachronic respects.

What has been said regarding the development of fundamental truths in the partner churches, and what was more precisely limited and emphasized in Thesis II, also applies to the community of faith as condition and presupposition for eucharistic fellowship.

These propositions have already been realized in the eucharistic fellowship with the *Orthodox churches*, which has already been approved—despite the remaining disagreements regarding the papacy, which, since Vatican I, has become not just a juridical and disciplinary issue, but a somewhat dogmatic one. One thing is certain: the Orthodox do not acknowledge a papacy in the specific Vatical I determined form of universal jurisdictional primacy. Nor, according to Ratzinger, should it be required of them. It is sufficient that they agree to a doctrine of the papacy like the one that existed during the first millennium, and that they acknowledge the pope as first in honor and as the presider over charity.[118]

However, this arrangement is also especially meaningful to the churches of the Reformation. For the dogma of universal jurisdictional primacy of the pope, and of the infallibility of his teaching office, is precisely the problem today still perceived to be the greatest obstacle between the churches. What has in the meantime been conceded to the Orthodox churches on this matter should also be equitable for the churches of the Reformation. That was perceived and formulated in precisely this way in the Anglican–Roman Catholic Dialogue.[119]

Moreover, Theses IVa and IVb, regarding the Petrine office and Petrine service as it is applied by the pope, have tried to show in what manner the partner churches are able to acknowledge the meaning and right of the Petrine service of the Roman pope to be the concrete guarantor of the Church in truth and love. Again Ratzinger's words should be taken into account: "The claim of truth should not be made when it is not forcefully and immovably valid. What is in reality a historically developed form, which is more or less intimately related to truth, must not be imposed as truth. Thus just when the full weight of truth and its indispensability is brought into play, it must conform to an integrity which is careful not to claim truth prematurely, and which is prepared to seek the inner dimensions of truth with the eyes of love."[120]

Eucharistic fellowship with the churches of the Reformation is generally considered impossible before Church unity, because of their alleged "*defectus ordinis*," however one wishes to translate this formulation—as lack of ordination or as lack of its fullness. This *defectus ordinis* is not simply considered irrelevant in our thesis. But, on the basis of many convergence and consensus papers on the ministerial office, it can be seen that the churches of the Reformation speak of the ministerial office and ordination through a "regular call (*rite vocatus*)"[121] so that the "deficiency of ordination" must, at the very least, be interpreted with great caution. A comparison of ordination liturgies in the partner churches moreover discloses an astonishing similarity of content and functional elements. They are the basis for a possible mutual recognition of ministerial office and ordination.[122]

Finally, if—as formulated in Thesis VII—all churches pledge themselves to perform ordinations with prayer and the laying-on of hands, then, with respect to ministerial office and ordination, the condition for possible pulpit and altar fellowship would clearly be met. The *defectus ordinis* would have been eliminated. We do not say that this is already the case in all partner churches, but we are signaling a possibility for the future which, we are convinced, is not utopian at all.

Another condition for pulpit and altar fellowship is the correct *administration of the Eucharist*: an ordained liturgist should preside over the celebration; the supper of Jesus should be made distinguishable in the way it is presented in the biblical reports and the words of institution; the "discerning the body" of the Lord (1 Cor. 11:29) should be safeguarded. This means that the Lord's Supper is not simply the continuation of Jesus' meal with tax collectors and sinners, but rather a unique event of a special kind—the sacramental representation, in the form of bread and wine, of His submission unto death for the life of the world; and of the fellowship of the disciples of Jesus occurring in the sign of the meal. That does not contradict a connection with Jesus' meal fellowship with tax collectors and sinners; rather, these are placed in the appropriate and larger context.

A feasible way to prepare and present full pulpit and altar fellowship would be to work on an ecumenical setting of liturgical texts for the church year, as well as of eucharistic prayers. This should not be impossible, since joint formulations of fundamental texts like the Lord's Prayer, the Apostles' Creed, and the Confession of Nicaea and Constantinople already exist.

An agreement regarding the handling of leftover *eucharistic elements* is also indispensable to full pulpit and altar fellowship. It must not be regarded as a special sign of Christian freedom to treat the elements with as little respect as possible and to profane them. No one can object if, following the celebration of the Lord's Supper, "a clean sweep" is made, and the leftover elements are consumed by the liturgist. But the meaning of reserving the elements in order to commune the sick should not be lost.[123] A practice customary in the Eastern churches could become adopted as common practice. It is true that, unlike the Roman Catholic church, the Eastern church does not possess a specifically eucharistic piety in the sense of meditations and processions, and in the sense of adoration of the "most holy." The partner churches need not adopt these forms for the sake of the unity of faith, but all the churches should respect them and appreciate them as legitimate development of the mystery given in the Lord's Supper. This also means that the forms of Catholic eucharistic piety and practice should not have the mark of a protest but rather the form of a faithful witness. Therefore they should be presented and performed in such a way that they offend no one who is a believer and well disposed.

III

On the basis of the fundamental statements as to the understanding of Eucharist and Church, the conclusion can be drawn that the *alternative*—Lord's Supper as sign and expression of already existing unity, or as sign effecting unity—is not legitimate. For the unity of faith and of the Church is not monolithic, static, or conceivable as definitely completed. It is open-ended and, as enduring and living unity, is marked by the incomplete, the "in transit," and by the eschatological reservation. One can also describe this ecclesiological state of affairs by defining the reality of the Church as gift *and* task; the unity appearing in the Eucharist can be understood as unity antecedently given through Jesus Christ, which becomes the constant and endless task for the community of those bound to Christ; it can be understood as striving for unity (see Eph. 4:13) and as endeavors toward unification and reconciliation.

The two great sacraments are assigned to these two aspects: the once-for-all baptism, and the continual celebration of the Eucharist. In the celebration of the Lord's Supper, which Jesus bequeathed as sign of His constant presence, as sign of unity with Him and therefore as sign of the unity of the participants in this meal with each other—in the ever-new accomplishment of this sign—those who through baptism have been irrevocably incorporated in the Church are admitted to the dynamics of unity which unites those who celebrate with God Himself by binding them to Jesus and to each other. Thus they partake more and more of His grace. The sign of ecclesiastical unity set in this accomplishment effects what it indicates precisely by being set as sign, and by both empowering and obligating the receiver to work for peace and unity.

The possibility thus opened up leads to a question one could formulate in this way: if the essence of the Lord's Supper is to further and to expedite the unification of those bound to Jesus and to each other through faith and baptism, why should it not also be particularly qualified to reestablish an ecclesiastical unity which is in fact broken? It will not be easy to avoid this consequence, especially if one is aware of the temporariness and fragility of all ecclesiastical unity vis-à-vis the eschatological termination, and if one knows that eucharistic fellowship can anticipate complete unity only in the sign of hope. This connection has already been established in the agreement with the churches of the East; broken unity is being mended and reestablished.[124]

Certain consequences regarding actual practice can *already* be derived from these basic conclusions. A general, all-inclusive, and continuous practice of eucharistic fellowship between the churches does not yet exist. Nor should it be practiced as self-evident until there is full ecclesiastical unity. There are reasons for this, namely, that the conditions do not yet exist for a possible full and continuous faith, church, pulpit, and eucharistic fellowship. A full eucharistic fellowship would implicitly deny that the separation of the churches has any theological significance at all.

But is the conclusion permitted that open communion, as expression of eucharistic hospitality, can be considered possible under no circumstances, in no conceivable situation whatever? Even after serious and responsible soul-searching, and with due consideration to all the circumstances and consequences, is it impossible because it would be tantamount to betraying one's own church? Is this matter therefore a case of all or nothing? This cannot be said when participants are unable to understand the actual circumstances and manner of eucharistic fellowship as a sign of indifference toward a wider and full unity of the church, and instead make of it a sign of the determined striving for the completion of unity.

The Synod of Bishops in the Federal Republic of Germany has taken a particular look at this situation, delineated it clearly, and then left it up to the conscientious decision and responsibility of the individual.[125] But even this kind of exception would not be possible, if there were only the present Catholic no to the Lord's Supper of other churches—with the exception of their attitude toward the Eastern church.

If fellowship at the Lord's table is viewed as expression and seal of unity, can it not be that sometimes, in faith and obedience, one may already anticipate the goal set before everyone? Can it not be that in certain ecumenical groups that have been growing in faith for years, or among the confessionally mixed marriage partners who do not consider their fellowship to be the misfortune of a mixed marriage but an ecumenical opportunity and obligation, there already exists that community in faith—even with regard to the real presence of Christ in the sacrament—which is considered to be the precondition for eucharistic hospitality?[126]

That is why this *kind* of participation in the Lord's Supper of another church, under the indicated conditions, is not a betrayal of one's own church. The pronouncements of the Protestant churches in Germany take this viewpoint into account in their regulations. The document *The Eucharist* states,

> The Lutheran church is also aware of the link between Eucharistic and church fellowship. Nevertheless, it recognizes, even in the present state of church division, a number of possibilities of Eucharistic fellowship. The criteria it employs enables it to acknowledge the validity of the Eucharistic celebration of others more freely than does the Roman Catholic church. Because of the already noted commonalities in the understanding of the gospel, which has decisive effects on proclamation, administration of the sacraments, and liturgical practice, the Lutherans feel that even now exchange of pulpits and common Eucharistic celebrations can on occasion be recommended. The Lutherans emphasized that the communion practices of the separated

churches must receive their orientation from that which is demanded of the church by the ministry of reconciliation among men. A celebration of the Lord's Supper in which baptized believers may not participate, suffers from an inner contradiction, and from the start, therefore, does not fulfill the purpose for which the Lord established it. (No. 73)[127]

IV

The paths to pulpit and altar fellowship have already been described in part. Attention should be drawn to a particular viewpoint; it too can be found in the document *The Eucharist*:

> The best way to unity in the Eucharistic celebration and fellowship is the renewal of the Eucharist itself in the different churches, in regard to teaching and liturgy.

Even with regard to the Eucharist it is steps taken toward the center that bring us closer together. A part of this is "that the faithful come to the holy liturgy with proper dispositions, that their thoughts match their words, and that they cooperate with divine grace, lest they receive it in vain" (no. 75).[128]

The required renewal must always aim at two things: first, the Lord, His Word, and His will; next, the contemporaries, with their difficulties and their potential—the "small herd" of fellow believers as well as the innumerable multitude of fellow human beings for whose salvation the Eucharist is intended.

The joint testimony of eucharistic faith and the joint attempt to do justice to it in life have nothing to do with uniformity. There is a wide choice in liturgical forms, just as there is in theology and in piety. They can, and should, illumine and complement each other. What applies to ecclesiastical life as a whole also applies to liturgical forms: "Thus in their diversity all bear witness to the admirable unity in the body of Christ. This very diversity of the gifts of grace, of ministries, and of work gathers the children of God into one, because 'all these things are work of the one and the same Spirit' " (1 Cor. 12:11) (no. 75).[129]

A greater commonality must be strived for without impairing this diversity. The following quotes the document *The Eucharist*:

According to common conviction, the eucharistic celebration forms a whole which includes a number of constitutive elements. Among these are: proclamation of the Word of God, thanksgiving for the acts of God in creation and redemption together with the remembering of the death and resurrection of Christ, the words of institution in accordance with the witness of the New Testament, the invocation of the Holy Spirit on bread and wine and on the congregation, intercession for the church and the world, the Lord's Prayer, and eating and drinking in communion with Christ and every member of the church.

Liturgical practice should correspond to this jointly affirmed fundamental pattern. In addition to the common tasks which this agreement implies, there are others which involve special challenge to our churches.

Lutherans are convinced that Catholics should seek:

1. the avoidance of celebrations of the Mass without participation of the people;
2. better use of the possibilities for proclamation within each celebration of the Eucharist;
3. the administration of Holy Communion under both species.

Catholics are convinced that Lutherans should seek:

1. more frequent celebrations of Holy Communion ("As the Eucharist is the new liturgical service Christ has given to the Church, it seems normal that it should be celebrated not less frequently than every Sunday, or once a week");
2. a greater participation by the congregation as a whole (particularly by children);
3. a closer link between liturgy of the word and liturgy of the sacrament.

It should be acknowledged that the differences in practice reflected in these diverse request are connected with continuing differences in the understanding of faith. We must join together in clarifying and overcoming them. (No. 76)[130]

V

There has already been much study of the *forms* of a pulpit and altar fellowship, and several models exist. The word "intercommunion" is not a particularly felicitous creation, since it means the reciprocal admission to the Lord's Supper of the other church. A more appropriate term would seem to be "open communion" or "mutual Eucharistic hospitality" (Bishop L. A. Elchinger). Intercelebration means the simultaneous celebration of the Lord's Supper—moreover in the same room—or the division of the words of institution into two liturgies, whereby the officials of the respective churches preside over the celebration. But the still-existing fact of separatedness becomes particularly painful and obvious in this model.

Pulpit and eucharistic fellowship, as far as and to the extent that it is already feasible, as a rule means that Christians can participate in another confession's celebration of the Lord's Supper—as is already provided for in the arrangement with the Eastern churches.

According to what has been said in this thesis so far, a pulpit and altar fellowship—even if not yet feasible with everyone—is nevertheless imminent and in certain cases already capable of being realized, although the churches are still separated and their liturgies are different. Therefore it is really obvious that, after they come together as partner churches of the one Church, they can and should have full pulpit and altar fellowship. Nor do they have to simply eliminate the differences in their liturgies, or allow them to melt into the Latin liturgy. Many of the details already mentioned, which were designated as preconditions for the realization of altar fellowship even before full union, can be applied to altar fellowship after unification.

Conclusion

Let us summarize the *principal ideas of all the theses.*

Our theses do not assert that full unity of faith and Church unity—with all the consequences—already exist. Instead, they intend to point out, not the utopian, but rather the actual conditions which can already be satisfied to achieve such a possibility. They intend to clarify the factual presuppositions under which one could achieve the unity for which Christians in all the churches have been praying for many years. How long it will take to honor this prayer we dare not say; but we would like to assert that we do not have too much time left to accomplish it. All the signs of the time favor it.

So that the goal can be reached, it is necessary that the reasons underlying our theses be received—above all the ecumenical documents from the whole world, especially the results of the dialogues about the Lord's Supper, about ministerial office and ordination, about the papacy and Petrine service; but also the diverse practical experiences at every level. Both the church leadership and the grass roots must receive them, for the ecumenical situation is different from congregation to congregation.

But it is important that not just a few pioneers in the field of ecumenical theology or a committed ecumenical practice set out and hurry ahead, though one must have them too. It is important to remain in touch with all the members of the people of God, to stay within calling and hearing distance, as it were, and to transmit to them the consciousness (and at the same time remove widespread fear) that the goal does not signify loss of continuity or indentity but instead means gaining both in far greater dimensions. Churches should remain churches and become *one* Church.

It is certainly correct to say that the work of unity of faith and unity of the Church, the goal of pulpit and altar fellowship, are the

139

gift of God, of His Christ, and of His Spirit. But it is not correct to say that, as is sometimes said, the gift occurs overnight and just appears out of the blue. Gift and grace do not exclude, they include the tasks imposed and the claims made on human beings. God works through people—through their commitment and their willingness. People can deny and close their minds to the call of grace and to the hour, to the signs of the time. People—expressed in human terms—have caused the separation of the Church into confessions. People can alter history and renew it; and they must do so if what happened was not good and if it brought harm and scandal.

The indispensable prayer to the Lord of the Church for the unity of Christians and of the churches must not be an alibi for human sloth and lack of imagination; instead, it must be the ever-new motivation to an attitude and mind-set which is expressed in the rule of Taizé: "Never be content with the scandal of separated Christendom. Have the passion for the unity of the body of Christ."

Notes

1. Lavigerie (1825–92) was the apostolic delegate for Central Africa since 1868. He advocated the integration of blacks in the mission church, and promoted national antislavery laws.

2. *Codex iuris canonici* (Vatican City: Vatican Library, 1983; English translation by the Canon Law Society of America, Washington, D.C., 1983).

3. Joseph Ratzinger, *Introduction to Christianity*, trans. J. R. Foster (New York: Herder & Herder, 1969), 52.

4. W. D. Hauschild, "Das trinitärische Dogma von 381 als Ergebnis verbindlicher Konsensbildung," in *Glaubensbekenntnis und Kirchengemeinschaft. Das Modell von Konstantinopel (381)*, ed. K. Lehmann and Wolfhart Pannenberg (Freiburg and Göttingen, 1982), 13.ʳ

5. A. Ganoczy, "Formale und inhaltliche Aspekte der mittelalterlichen Konzilien als Zeichen kirchlichen Ringens um ein universales Glaubensbekenntnis," in *Glaubensbekenntnis und Kirchengemeinschaft*, ed. Lehmann and Pannenberg, 55 n. 2.

6. Hauschild, "Das trinitärische Dogma," 48.

7. "Pastorale Zusammenarbeit der Kirchen im Dienst an der christlichen Einheit," 3.2.1, in *Gemeinsame Synode der Bistümer in der Bundesrepublik Deutschland. Beschlüsse der Vollversammlung. Offizielle Gesamtausgabe* I (Freiburg, Basel, Vienna, 1976), 780.

8. Wolfhart Pannenberg, "Die Bedeutung des Bekenntnisses von Nicäa-Konstantinopel für den ökumenischen Dialog heute," *Ökumenische Rundschau* 31 (1982): 129–40. See also idem, "Faith and Order in der ökumenische Bewegung," in ibid., 47–59, esp. 53.

9. See also Ganoczy, "Aspekte der mittelalterlichen Konzilien," 78.

10. *Decree on Ecumenism (Unitatis Redintegratio)*, no. 11. English translation in *Documents of Vatican II*, ed. Walter M. Abbott and Joseph Gallagher. Hereafter cited Abbott. (New York: Association Press, 1966), 354.

11. Pannenberg, "Faith and Order," 54.

12. *Dogmatic Constitution of the Church (Lumen Gentium)*, no. 4. Abbott, 16–17.

13. Ibid., no. 15. Abbott, 34.

14. Walter Kasper, "Die Kirche als Sakrament des Geistes," in *Kirche –*

141

Ort des Geistes, ed. Walter Kasper and G. Sauter (Freiburg, Basel, Vienna, 1976), 13–55.

15. *Pastoral Constitution on the Church in the Modern World (Gaudium et Spes),* no. 4. Abbott, 201–3.

16. *Decree on Ecumenism,* no. 3. Abbott, 346.

17. Heinrich J. Denzinger, *Enchiridion Symbolorum,* 36th ed. (Freiburg: Herder, 1976). Hereafter cited DS.

18. Abbott, 32.

19. Ibid., 357–58.

20. Ibid., 359–60.

21. Ibid., 360.

22. Ibid., 360–61.

23. Original texts in *Die Bekenntnisschriften der evangelisch-lutherischen Kirche,* 3d ed., rev. (Göttingen: Vandenhoeck & Ruprecht, 1956), 66–67, 97–100. Hereafter cited BS. English text in Theodore G. Tappert, ed. and trans., *The Book of Concord* (Philadelphia: Fortress Press, 1959), 34–35, 61–63. Hereafter cited BC.

24. Smalcald Articles, 1537. Part II, 4 (The Papacy). BS 427–33. BC 298–301. See also Remigius Bäumer, *Martin Luther und der Papst* (Münster, 1970).

25. Apology of the Augsburg Confession VII, 23. BS 239. BC 172.

26. See R. Aubert, *Vatikanum I* (Mainz, 1965).

27. DS 3050–75.

28. DS 3112–17.

29. Peter Brunner, "Reform—Reformation—Einst—Heute," *Kerygma und Dogma* 13 (1967): 159–83.

30. Not in the final text of the *Dogmatic Constitution of the Church (Lumen Gentium).* Abbott, 16–17.

31. Hans U. von Balthasar, *Der antirömische Affekt* (Freiburg, Basel, Vienna, 1974).

32. A. Vögtle, "Petrus," in *Lexikon für Theologie und Kirche,* ed. Josef Höfer and Karl Rahner, 2d. ed., rev. (Freiburg: Herder, 1957–65), 334–40. Hereafter cited LTHK.

33. Ibid., 338–39.

34. P. Stockmeier, "Das Petrusamt in der frühen Kirche," in *Zum Thema Petrusamt und Papsttum* (Stuttgart, 1970).

35. W. de Vries, *Papsttum als ökumenische Frage* (Munich and Mainz, 1979), 146.

36. Walter Kasper, "Das Petrusamt in ökumenischer Perspektive," in *In der Nachfolge Jesus Christi: Zum Besuch des Papstes* (Freiburg, Basel, Vienna, 1980).

37. Harding Meyer in *Papsttum und Petrusdienst,* ed. H. Stirnimann and Lukas Vischer (Frankfurt, 1975), 76.

38. Heinrich Fries, "Sind die Erwartungen erfüllt?" in *Karl Rahner— Oskar Cullmann—Heinrich Fries* (Munich, 1966), 69-70.

39. Joseph Ratzinger, "Das Ende der Bannflüche von 1054. Folgen für Rom und die Ostkirchen," *Internationale katholische Zeitschrift* 4 (1974): 289-303.

40. Abbott, 358-59.

41. *Herder-Korrespondenz* 30 (1976): 67.

42. Joseph Ratzinger, "Die ökumenische Situation—Orthodoxie, Katholizismus und Reformation," in *Theologische Prinzipienlehre* (Munich, 1982), 209.

43. German text in Harding Meyer, *Luthertum und Katholizismus im Gespräch. Ergebnisse und Stand der katholisch-lutherischen Dialoge in USA und auf Weltebene* (Frankfurt, 1973), 143-74. English text, "The Gospel and the Church," Report of the Joint Roman-Lutheran Study Commission in *Lutheran World* 19, no. 3 (1972): 1-15.

44. Paul C. Empie and T. Austin Murphy, eds., *Papal Primacy and the Universal Church* (Minneapolis: Augsburg, 1974), 19-23.

45. Translation based on text in ibid., 22-23.

46. Ibid., 23.

47. Paul C. Empie, T. Austin Murphy, and Joseph A. Burgess, eds., *Teaching Authority and the Infallibility of the Church* (Minneapolis: Augsburg, 1978), 14.

48. *Evangelischer Erwachsenenkatechismus* (Gütersloh, 1977), 916.

49. Wolfhart Pannenberg, "Einheit der Kirche als Glaubenswirklichkeit und als ökumenisches Ziel," *Una Sancta* 30 (1975): 220-21.

50. German text in *Herder-Korrespondenz* 36 (1982): 288-93. English text in *The Final Report* (London: SPCK and Catholic Truth Society, 1982; Cincinnati: Forward Movement Publications; and Washington, D.C.: USA Catholic Conference, 1982) Translation is based on the English text. Introduction, no. 6, p. 7.

51. Ibid., no. 9, p. 8.

52. *Authority in the Church II*, no. 9, p. 85.

53. Ibid., p. 86.

54. Ibid., pp. 87-88.

55. Elucidation, no. 8, p. 76.

56. Ibid., pp. 89-90.

57. Ibid., p. 90.

58. Ibid., p. 92.

59. Ibid., p. 93.

60. Ibid.

61. Ibid.

62. Ibid., pp. 94-95.

63. Ibid., p. 60.

64. Ibid., no. 33, p. 97.

65. Summarized on the basis of F. Wolfinger, "Die Rezeption theologischer Einsichten und ihre theologische und ökumenische Bedeutung," *Catholica* 31 (1977): 204.

66. Abbott, 49.

67. KNA Interview on 15 April 1982.

68. Abbott, 49.

69. See Heinrich Fries, "Ex sese, non ex consensu ecclesiae," in *Volk Gottes. Zum Kirchenverständnis der katholischen, evangelischen und anglikanischen Theologie,* ed. Remigius Bäumer and H. Dolch (Freiburg, 1967), 480–500.

70. Augsburg Confession, 1530, XXVIII. BS 120–33. BC 81–94. Apology of the Augsburg Confession, XIV. BS 296–97. BC 214–15. Smalcald Articles, 1537. Part III, 10. BS 457–58. BC 314.

71. Abbott, 53.

72. BS 123:21–124:22. BC 84:21–22.

73. In *Amt, Ämter, Dienste, Ordination. Ergebnis eines theologischen Gespräches,* ed. Joachim Rogge and H. Zeddies (Berlin, 1982), 62.

74. Walter Kasper, "Zur Frage der Anerkennung der Ämter in den lutherischen Kirchen," *Theologische Quartalschrift* 151 (1971): 103.

75. "The Hierarchical Structure of the Church, With Special Reference to the Episcopate." Abbott, 37–56.

76. Ibid., 52–53.

77. See the declaration of the German bishops in 1875 against Bismarck's executive order. DS 3112–16.

78. Abbott, 40.

79. Ibid., 47.

80. Ibid., 46.

81. Ibid., 48.

82. Ibid.

83. Ibid., 51.

84. Yves Congar, "Tatsachen, Probleme und Betrachtungen hinsichtlich der Weihevollmacht und der Beziehungen zwischen Presbyterat und dem Episkopat," in *Heilige Kirche* (Stuttgart, 1966), 283–316.

85. *The Ministry in the Church,* Roman Catholic–Lutheran Joint Commission (Geneva: Lutheran World Federation, 1982), 20.

86. Ibid., 21.

87. *Baptism, Eucharist and Ministry,* Faith and Order Paper, no. 111 (Geneva: World Council of Churches, 1982), "Ministry," 29–30.

88. Walter Kasper, "Ökumenischer Fortschritt im Amtsverständnis?" in *Amt im Widerstreit,* ed. K. Schuh (Berlin, 1973), 57–58.

89. *The Ministry in the Church,* no. 63, p. 25.

90. Ibid., no. 77, p. 29.

91. Abbott, 364.
92. *The Ministry in the Church*, no. 77, p. 29.
93. Ibid., 30–31.
94. *Baptism, Eucharist and Ministry*, 29.
95. Edmund Schlink, "Die apostolische Sukzession und die Gemeinschaft der Ämter," in *Reform und Anerkennung kirchlicher Ämter. Ein Memorandum der Arbeitsgemeinschaft ökumenischer Universitätsinstitute* (Munich and Mainz, 1973), 155.
96. K. Mörsdorf, *Lehrbuch des Kirchenrechts I* (Munich, Paderborn, Vienna, 1964), 499. On the whole theme, see "Ortskirche und Bischofswahl," *Concilium* 16 (1980), Heft 8/9.
97. Abbott, 47.
98. Karl Rahner, "Reform der Bischofswahl," *Stimmen der Zeit* 107 (1982): 289.
99. P. Stockmeier, "Die Wahl des Bischofs durch Klerus und Volk in der frühen Kirche," *Concilium* 16 (1980): 466.
100. K. Mörsdorf, "Bischof," in LTHK II (1958): 502.
101. *Decree on the Bishops' Pastoral Office in the Church*. Abbott, 411.
102. C. Cereti, "Die ökumenische Bedeutung einer Mitwirkung der Gläubigen bei der Bischofswahl," *Concilium* 16 (1980): 497.
103. Ibid.
104. P. Lengsfeld and H. G. Stobbe, *Theologischer Konsens und Kirchenspaltung* (Stuttgart, Berlin, Cologne, Mainz, 1981), esp. 126–34.
105. *The Eucharist*, Roman Catholic–Lutheran Joint Commission (Geneva: Lutheran World Federation, 1980), no. 72, p. 25.
106. *Decree on Ecumenism*, no. 8. Abbott, 352. See also Johannes Brosseder, "Abendmahlsgemeinschaft als Weg zur Kirchengemeinschaft?" in *Auf Wegen der Versöhnung*, ed. P. Neuner and F. Wolfinger, (Frankfurt, 1982), 220–30.
107. Abbott, 16.
108. *Ways to Community*, Roman Catholic–Lutheran Joint Commission (Geneva: Lutheran World Federation, 1981), 22.
109. *Constitution on the Sacred Liturgy (Sacrosanctum Concilium)*, no. 7. Abbott, 140–41.
110. The Leuenberg Concord of 1971 represents an agreement of ninety Lutheran and Reformed churches from sixteen countries (excluding the North American continent). Text in *Lutherische Monatshefte* 12 (1972): 271–74.
111. Abbott, 20.
112. Ibid., 28.
113. Ibid., 363–64.
114. Ibid., 34.
115. Ibid., 364.

116. See K. Lehmann and Edmund Schlink, eds., *Das Opfer Jesu Christi und seine Gegenwart in der Kirche. Klärungen zum Opfercharakter des Herrenmahles* (Freiburg and Göttingen, 1983).

117. *The Eucharist*, 20.

118. Joseph Ratzinger, "Zur Frage der Wiedervereinigung zwischen Ost und West," in *Theologische Erkenntnislehre* (Munich, 1982), 209.

119. See Heinrich Fries, "Das Petrusamt im anglikanisch-katholischen Dialog," *Stimmen der Zeit* 107 (1982): 723–38.

120. Ratzinger, "Zur Frage der Wiedervereinigung, 208.

121. Augsburg Confession XIV. BS 69. BC 36.

122. See the comprehensive discussion of H. Schütte, *Amt, Ordination und Sukzession im Verständnis evangelischer und katholischer Exegeten und Dogmatiker der Gegenwart sowie in Dokumenten ökumenischer Gespräche* (Düsseldorf, 1974); Karl Rahner, *Vorfragen zu einem ökumenischen Amtsverständnis* (Freiburg, Basel, Vienna, 1974).

123. See Harding Meyer and Vinzenz Pfnür, "The Presence of Christ in the Eucharist," in *The Eucharist*, Supplementary Study, 61–65.

124. See Heinrich Fries, *Ein Glaube, eine Taufe—getrennt beim Abendmahl?* (Graz, Vienna, Cologne, 1971), 67–69.

125. "Beschluss Gottesdienst," 5.5. *Offizielle Gesamtausgabe*, 216.

126. Heinrich Fries, "Die Kirche im ökumenischen Dialog," in *Die Kirche Jesu Christi. Enttäuschung und Hoffnung*, ed. P. Gordan (Graz, Vienna, Cologne, Kevelaer, 1982), 269–70.

127. *The Eucharist*, 26.

128. Ibid.

129. Ibid., 27.

130. Ibid., 27–28.